Leveraging
GEN-AI & GPT for
Consultants©

A comprehensive guide for setting up or enhancing an already-existing consulting

business with/for Generative AI

Table of Contents

Chapter 1

Introduction - Understanding Generative AI Consulting

Objective and Purpose

Welcome to "Leveraging GEN-AI & GPT for Consultants." This book aims to equip you with the knowledge and tools needed to excel in the burgeoning field of generative AI consulting. As artificial intelligence (AI) continues to transform industries, the demand for expertise in integrating AI solutions has surged. It doesn't matter if you are trying to set up or enhance an already existing consulting business, this book is designed to bridge the gap between theoretical understanding and practical application, providing you with actionable insights to offer high-value consulting services.

The primary objective of this book is to help you:

- Understand the fundamental concepts of generative AI.
- Identify opportunities to leverage AI in various industries.
- Develop a strategic approach to consulting with AI technologies.
- Master the practical aspects of setting up and running a successful AI consulting practice.

What problem are we solving?

In today's rapidly evolving business landscape, organizations encounter significant challenges when it comes to harnessing the power of generative AI technology. Limited resources often restrict their ability to invest in expensive AI infrastructure and hire top AI talent, hindering their progress in adopting generative AI solutions. Moreover, organizations must navigate a highly competitive market, where attracting and retaining skilled AI professionals is a constant struggle. Additionally, shrinking budgets pose further constraints on their ability to explore and implement cutting-edge AI technologies.

Why now?

Why is now the right time to leverage this new AI technology in your consulting practice? The global AI consulting services market is segmented into service type, enterprise size, and industry vertical. The service type segment is bifurcated into automation consulting, analytics consulting, digital transformation strategy formulation, and others. Among the service type, the digital transformation strategy formulation segment is expected to account for moderate revenue share in the target segment. The enterprise size segment is divided into small- and medium-sized enterprises (SMEs) and large enterprises. Among the enterprise size, the large enterprise segment is expected to account for **major** revenue share in the global market.

Market Size

The expanding market for generative AI training and support encompasses a wide range of industries, including consultants, sole proprietors, and enterprise-level corporate clients.

According to a report by *Grand View Research*, the global artificial intelligence market size was valued at approximately USD 62.35 billion in 2020 and is projected to grow at a compound annual growth rate (CAGR) of around 40% from 2021 to 2028. While this figure represents the broader AI market, it indicates the overall growth potential for AI-related services, including generative AI training and support.

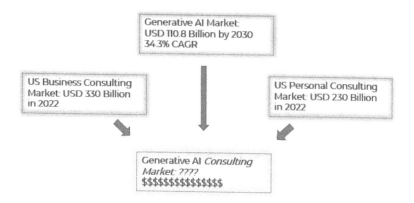

Market Potential

The demand for generative AI training and support is driven by challenges in recruitment, talent retention, operations, capital management, administration, time management, and marketing strategies.

The market size for generative AI training and support *consulting* is expected to be significant, considering the increasing adoption of AI technologies across industries and the growing demand for AI-driven solutions. Generative AI has the potential to revolutionize sectors such as marketing, healthcare, finance, manufacturing, and more.

Trained and industry-experienced consultants are poised to capture a significant share of the generative AI training and support market by providing tangible evidence of the transformative impact of generative AI services and highlighting the value they can bring to their clients.

Generative AI Value Chain

As the development and deployment of generative AI systems gets under way, a new value chain is emerging to support the training and use of this powerful technology. The opportunity size for new entrants in Services and Training is second only to End-User Applications.

There are opportunities across the generative AI value chain, but the most significant is building end-user applications.

Generative AI value chain

Opportunity size for new entrants in next 3–5 years, scale of 1–5

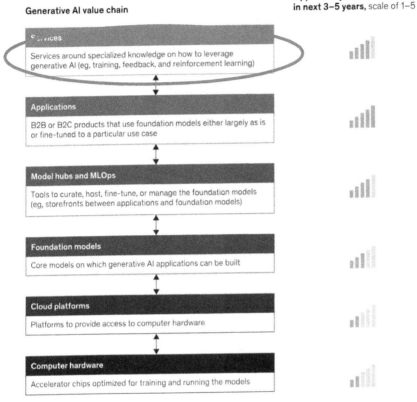

Services

Services around specialized knowledge on how to leverage generative AI (eg, training, feedback, and reinforcement learning)

Applications

B2B or B2C products that use foundation models either largely as is or fine-tuned to a particular use case

Model hubs and MLOps

Tools to curate, host, fine-tune, or manage the foundation models (eg, storefronts between applications and foundation models)

Foundation models

Core models on which generative AI applications can be built

Cloud platforms

Platforms to provide access to computer hardware

Computer hardware

Accelerator chips optimized for training and running the models

McKinsey & Company

Importance of Industry-Specific Experience

While AI has universal applications, its impact can vary significantly across different industries. Industry-specific experience is crucial because it allows you to tailor AI solutions to the unique challenges and requirements of each sector. For instance, AI applications in healthcare might focus on predictive analytics for patient outcomes, while in finance, the emphasis could be on algorithmic trading or fraud detection.

As a consultant, your role is to bridge the gap between AI technology and industry-specific needs. This requires a deep understanding of the industry you are consulting for, including its regulatory environment, competitive landscape, and operational challenges. Combining this knowledge with your AI expertise will enable you to deliver more relevant, effective, and impactful solutions.

Benefits of Generative AI in Consulting

Generative AI, a subset of AI that focuses on creating new content, designs, or solutions, offers numerous benefits in the consulting realm:

- **Innovation and Creativity**: Generative AI can produce novel solutions, designs, and ideas that might not be immediately apparent through traditional approaches.
- **Efficiency and Productivity**: Automating repetitive tasks and generating high-quality outputs quickly can significantly enhance productivity.
- **Personalization**: AI can tailor solutions to individual client needs, offering a more customized and relevant service.
- **Data-Driven Insights**: AI algorithms can analyze vast amounts of data to uncover insights that inform strategic decision-making.

Structure of the Book

This book is structured to guide you through the entire journey of becoming a successful generative AI consultant. Each chapter builds on the previous one, gradually expanding your knowledge and skills. Here's a brief overview of what you can expect:

1. **Understanding Generative AI Consulting**: Introduction to the role, responsibilities, and ethical considerations of a generative AI consultant.

2. **Setting Up Your Generative AI Consulting Service**: Guidance on defining your services, building a brand, and navigating legal considerations.

3. **Building a Knowledge Base and Skill Sets**: Resources and tools to stay updated with the latest technologies and research.

4. **Identifying Client Needs and Opportunities**: The ability to accurately identify client needs and uncover opportunities for generative AI is essential for a successful consulting practice.

5. **Crafting Tailored AI Solutions Using GPT Tools**: This chapter will guide you through the process of leveraging GPT tools to craft customized AI solutions.

6. **Using GPT in the Consulting Process for Generative AI Implementation**: A detailed look at the consulting process, with actionable steps and examples.

7. **Leveraging GPT for Business Planning for AI Consultants**: Incorporating GPT into your consulting business planning starts with defining clear goals and objectives.

8. **Marketing and Promoting Your Generative AI Services**: Creating a marketing strategy, building an online presence, and effective advertising.

9. **Working Efficiently and Prioritizing Projects**: Time management, project prioritization, and collaboration tools.

10. **Scaling and Growing Your Generative AI Business**: Strategies for scaling, hiring, and sustainable growth.

11. **Managing Business Risk and Ensuring Profitability**: Risk management, data privacy, and maximizing profitability.

12. **The Future of Generative AI Consulting**: Emerging trends, lifelong learning, and adapting to industry changes.

13. **Conclusion**: Recap of key points and final thoughts.

Throughout this book, we will utilize a methodology where we will first provide detailed descriptions of the subject matter, then provide practical examples, and finally give you "actionable insights" that will lead you, step-by-step, to develop your own outline for developing yourself and your consulting practice. By the end of this book, you will be well-equipped to navigate the complexities of AI consulting and deliver high-impact solutions to your clients.

Chapter 2

Setting Up Your Generative AI Consulting Service

In this chapter, we will guide you through the essential steps to establish a robust and reputable generative AI consulting service. You will learn how to define your service offerings, build a strong brand identity, and navigate the legal and regulatory landscape specific to generative AI consulting.

Defining Your Consulting Service Offerings

The first step in setting up your generative AI consulting service is to clearly define the specific services you will offer. This involves identifying your target audience, understanding their needs, and tailoring your offerings accordingly.

There are two broad categories of consulting services, each with overlap: **business consulting** and **consumer consulting**. We will be focusing on the larger group: business consulting. For a detailed listing of both consumer and business consulting specialties/industries, please see *Appendix 2: GenAI Consulting Fields.*

In addition to a specialty, a business consulting service may decide to specialize in one of two approaches to advising clients. The service may *emphasize the resolution of an issue* or *the transfer of needed skills to the client.* For example, a restaurant with cash flow problems may only need advice on how to resolve that specific problem. Or the owner may need to be trained in advanced cash flow forecasting and other aspects of business management.

There are advantages and disadvantages to both approaches for the consultant and the client. Problem resolution is less expensive for the client, but it may not solve the underlying cause. Skill transfer is more expensive for the client, but it reduces dependence on the consultant

Identifying and Defining Specific Services

Generative AI is a versatile technology that can be applied across various industries. Here are some common service offerings you might consider:

1. Model Development: Creating custom generative AI models tailored to specific business needs, such as natural language generation, image synthesis, or predictive analytics.
2. Model Deployment: Implementing and integrating AI models into existing business workflows, ensuring they operate smoothly and deliver the intended value.
3. Model Optimization: Enhancing the performance of existing AI models by fine-tuning algorithms, improving accuracy, and reducing computational costs.
4. Consultation and Training: Providing expert advice on AI strategy, conducting workshops, and training sessions to educate clients on the benefits and usage of generative AI.
5. Data Preparation and Management: Assisting clients in gathering, cleaning, and organizing their data to ensure it is suitable for AI applications.

Determining Your Target Audience

To tailor your services effectively, you need to identify your target audience. Consider the following steps:

1. Market Research: Conduct thorough research to understand the industries and sectors that can benefit most from generative AI. Look for sectors with high data availability and a strong need for automation and innovation.
2. Client Personas: Develop detailed client personas to represent different segments of your target audience. Include information such as industry, company size, key challenges, and potential use cases for generative AI.
3. Competitive Analysis: Analyze your competitors to identify gaps in their offerings that you can fill. Look for unique value propositions that can set your services apart.

Building a Strong Brand Identity

A strong brand identity is crucial for establishing credibility and attracting clients. Your brand should convey your expertise, values, and the unique benefits you offer.

Developing a Unique Value Proposition

Your value proposition should clearly articulate why clients should choose your services over competitors. Consider the following elements:

1. Core Benefits: Highlight the core benefits of your services, such as improved efficiency, cost savings, innovation, and competitive advantage.
2. Unique Selling Points: Identify what makes your services unique. This could be your specialized expertise, proprietary technology, or a proven track record of successful projects.
3. Client Testimonials and Case Studies: Use testimonials and case studies to showcase the positive impact of your services on previous clients. This provides social proof and builds trust with potential clients.

Creating a Compelling Brand Story and Messaging

Your brand story should resonate with your target audience and reflect your mission and values. Follow these steps:

1. Mission Statement: Craft a mission statement that reflects your commitment to helping clients leverage generative AI for success.
2. Brand Narrative: Develop a brand narrative that tells the story of your journey, your passion for AI, and how you have helped clients overcome challenges.
3. Consistent Messaging: Ensure your messaging is consistent across all channels, including your website, social media, and marketing materials. Use clear and concise language that communicates your expertise and value.

Legal and Regulatory Considerations for a Generative AI Startup

Navigating the legal and regulatory landscape is crucial for ensuring compliance and protecting your business.

Understanding the Legal and Ethical Frameworks

Generative AI raises several legal and ethical issues that you need to address:

1. Data Privacy: Ensure compliance with data privacy regulations, such as GDPR and CCPA. Implement robust data protection measures to safeguard client data.
2. Intellectual Property: Understand the intellectual property rights related to AI models and algorithms. Ensure that you have the necessary permissions to use any third-party data or technology.
3. Algorithmic Transparency: Be transparent about how your AI models work and the data they use. This helps build trust with clients and ensures compliance with regulations that require explainability.

Complying with Relevant Regulations and Standards

Compliance is essential to avoid legal issues and build a reputable business. Consider the following steps:

1. Regulatory Research: Stay updated on the latest regulations and standards related to generative AI. This includes industry-specific regulations that may apply to your clients.
2. Legal Counsel: Consult with legal experts who specialize in AI and technology to ensure your business practices comply with relevant laws.
3. Ethical Guidelines: Develop and adhere to ethical guidelines for AI use. This includes ensuring fairness, avoiding bias, and prioritizing the well-being of clients and end-users.

Actionable Insights and Examples

To make these concepts more tangible, let's explore some actionable insights and examples.

Case Study: Defining Consulting Services

Imagine you are setting up a generative AI consulting service focused on the healthcare industry. Here's how you might define your services:

1. Model Development: Create AI models that predict patient outcomes based on historical data, helping doctors make informed decisions.

2. Model Deployment: Integrate these models into hospital management systems to streamline operations and improve patient care.

3. Consultation and Training: Offer workshops for healthcare professionals to understand and utilize AI tools effectively.

Example: Crafting a Unique Value Proposition

Your unique value proposition for the healthcare sector could be:

"We provide cutting-edge generative AI solutions that enhance patient care, streamline hospital operations, and reduce costs. Our proprietary algorithms have been proven to improve diagnostic accuracy by 20%, ensuring better outcomes for patients and healthcare providers alike."

Example: Legal Compliance

To ensure compliance with data privacy regulations, you might implement the following measures:

1. Data Encryption: Use advanced encryption techniques to protect patient data.

2. Access Controls: Implement strict access controls to ensure that only authorized personnel can access sensitive information.

3. Regular Audits: Conduct regular audits to identify and address any potential vulnerabilities in your data management practices.

By following the guidelines and examples provided in this chapter, you can establish a strong foundation for your generative AI consulting service. Defining your offerings, building a compelling brand, and ensuring legal compliance are crucial steps in building a successful and reputable business.

Chapter 3

Building a Knowledge Base and Skill Set

To become a successful generative AI consultant, you need a solid foundation in the necessary knowledge and skills. This chapter will guide you through acquiring a deeper understanding of generative AI, mastering essential tools and technologies, and developing effective consulting skills.

Understanding the Fundamentals of Generative AI

Before diving into advanced topics, it's crucial to understand the core principles of generative AI. This includes learning about its underlying concepts, different types of generative models, and their applications.

Core Concepts and Terminology

1. Generative Models: Learn about the types of models that can generate new data similar to the input data they were trained on. This includes understanding the differences between discriminative and generative models.
2. Neural Networks: Gain a solid understanding of neural networks, the building blocks of generative AI models. This includes concepts like neurons, layers, activation functions, and backpropagation.
3. Training and Inference: Understand the processes involved in training generative models (adjusting model parameters based on training data) and inference (using the trained model to generate new data).

Types of Generative Models

1. Generative Adversarial Networks (GANs): Learn about GANs, where two neural networks (a generator and a discriminator) compete in a zero-sum game to produce realistic data.
2. Variational Autoencoders (VAEs): Study VAEs, which use probabilistic graphical models to encode input data into a latent space and then decode it back to generate new data.
3. Transformers: Understand transformer models, which have revolutionized natural language processing (NLP) with their ability to handle long-range dependencies in sequential data.

Applications of Generative AI

Explore various applications of generative AI across different industries:

1. Image Generation: Creating realistic images from textual descriptions or generating new artistic images.
2. Text Generation: Developing chatbots, writing assistants, and content generators.
3. Audio and Music Generation: Producing music, generating voiceovers, and creating sound effects.
4. Drug Discovery: Designing new molecules and predicting their properties for pharmaceutical applications.

Mastering Essential Tools and Technologies

To implement generative AI solutions, it is helpful to become familiar (preferably proficient) in the tools and technologies commonly used in the field. This does not mean that you have to study to become a data scientist, but you should know what a data scientist is, what they do, and what tools they use. As AI technologies progress, the easier it is to leverage new technologies without being a technical expert.

Programming Languages

1. Python: Python is the primary programming language for AI development due to its simplicity and extensive libraries. Learn how to use Python for data manipulation, model development, and deployment.
2. R: While less common than Python, R is valuable for statistical analysis and data visualization. Consider learning R if you work in research-heavy environments.

AI Frameworks and Libraries

1. TensorFlow: Developed by Google, TensorFlow is a powerful framework for building and deploying machine learning models. Learn how to create and train neural networks using TensorFlow.
2. PyTorch: PyTorch, developed by Facebook, is another popular framework known for its flexibility and ease of use. It is widely used in research and production environments.
3. Keras: Keras is a high-level neural networks API that runs on top of TensorFlow. It simplifies the process of building and training models, making it ideal for beginners.
4. Hugging Face Transformers: For NLP tasks, the Hugging Face Transformers library provides pre-trained models and tools for fine-tuning and deploying transformer models.

Cloud Platforms and Tools

1. AWS: Amazon Web Services offers a range of AI services and tools, such as SageMaker for building, training, and deploying machine learning models.
2. Google Cloud: Google Cloud Platform provides AI and machine learning services, including AutoML for custom model training and deployment.
3. Azure: Microsoft Azure offers AI services and tools, such as Azure Machine Learning, for building and deploying models at scale.

Developing Effective Consulting Skills

In addition to technical expertise, successful generative AI consultants need strong consulting skills. This includes understanding how to communicate with clients, manage projects, and provide actionable recommendations.

Communication Skills

1. Active Listening: Develop the ability to listen actively to clients, understand their needs, and ask pertinent questions.
2. Clear Communication: Learn to explain complex technical concepts in simple terms that clients can understand. Use visual aids and analogies to make your explanations more relatable.
3. Presentation Skills: Hone your presentation skills to effectively communicate your findings and recommendations to clients.

Practice using slides, demos, and interactive elements to engage your audience.

Project Management

1. Planning and Organization: Learn how to plan and organize projects, set realistic timelines, and allocate resources efficiently.
2. Agile Methodologies: Familiarize yourself with Agile project management methodologies, such as Scrum and Kanban, to manage AI projects effectively.
3. Risk Management: Develop strategies for identifying and mitigating risks associated with AI projects, such as data privacy concerns, model accuracy issues, and project delays.

Problem-Solving and Analytical Thinking

1. Analytical Skills: Enhance your ability to analyze data, identify patterns, and draw meaningful insights. Use statistical techniques and data visualization tools to support your analysis.
2. Creative Problem-Solving: Cultivate creative problem-solving skills to develop innovative solutions to complex challenges. Encourage brainstorming and collaboration to generate new ideas.
3. Decision-Making: Learn to make informed decisions based on data and evidence. Evaluate different options, consider potential outcomes, and choose the best course of action.

Actionable Insights and Examples

To help you apply the knowledge and skills covered in this chapter, here are some actionable insights and examples:

Example: Understanding Generative Models

Consider a scenario where you are tasked with developing a generative AI model for creating realistic human faces. Here's how you might approach it:

1. Model Selection: Choose a GAN as your generative model due to its effectiveness in image generation tasks.
2. Data Collection: Gather a large dataset of human faces, ensuring diversity in age, gender, ethnicity, and facial expressions.

3. Model Training: Use TensorFlow or PyTorch to build and train your GAN on the collected dataset. Monitor the training process to ensure the generator and discriminator are learning effectively.
4. Evaluation and Fine-Tuning: Evaluate the quality of the generated faces using metrics like the Fréchet Inception Distance (FID). Fine-tune the model parameters to improve the realism of the generated faces.

Actionable Insight: Mastering AI Frameworks

To master AI frameworks, follow these steps:

1. Online Courses: Enroll in online courses and tutorials that cover TensorFlow, PyTorch, and other relevant frameworks. Websites like Coursera, Udacity, and edX offer comprehensive courses on AI and machine learning.
2. Hands-On Practice: Work on practical projects and experiments to apply what you learn. Build and train different types of generative models to gain hands-on experience.
3. Community Engagement: Join online communities and forums, such as GitHub, Stack Overflow, and Reddit, to seek help, share knowledge, and stay updated on the latest advancements.

Example: Developing Consulting Skills

Imagine you are consulting for a retail company that wants to use generative AI to personalize customer experiences. Here's how you might apply your consulting skills:

1. Active Listening: Conduct initial meetings with key stakeholders to understand their goals, challenges, and expectations. Ask questions to clarify their needs and gather detailed requirements.
2. Clear Communication: Explain the potential of generative AI in personalizing customer experiences, using simple language and real-world examples. Highlight how AI can analyze customer data to generate personalized product recommendations.
3. Project Management: Develop a project plan outlining the key phases, milestones, and deliverables. Use Agile methodologies to manage the project, ensuring regular check-ins and progress updates with the client.

4. Problem-Solving: Identify potential challenges, such as data quality issues and integration with existing systems. Develop strategies to address these challenges, such as data cleaning techniques and API integrations.
5. Decision-Making: Recommend the best generative AI model for the task, considering factors like accuracy, scalability, and ease of deployment. Provide evidence-based justifications for your recommendations.

By building a strong knowledge base and skill set, you can position yourself as a competent and credible generative AI consultant. Mastering the technical aspects of generative AI and developing effective consulting skills will enable you to deliver high-value solutions to your clients and drive their success.

Chapter 4

Identifying Client Needs and Opportunities

The ability to accurately identify client needs and uncover opportunities for generative AI is essential for a successful consulting practice. This chapter will guide you through the process of understanding client requirements, conducting effective needs assessments, and discovering opportunities to apply generative AI for maximum impact.

Conducting Needs Assessments

Understanding client needs is the foundation of any successful consulting engagement. Often, a client may not even know that they need something. It is your job as the AI consultant to identify emerging opportunities (and potential risks, if they take no action). Conducting thorough needs assessments will help you gather the necessary information to tailor your solutions effectively.

Initial Consultations

1. Setting Up Initial Meetings: Arrange meetings with key stakeholders to discuss their goals, challenges, and expectations. Ensure all relevant decision-makers are present to get a comprehensive understanding of the organization's needs.
2. Effective Questioning Techniques: Use open-ended questions to encourage detailed responses. Examples include:
    o   "What are your main business objectives for the next year?"
    o   "What challenges are you currently facing that you think AI might help solve?"

- o   "Can you describe your current processes and where you see potential for improvement?"

3. Active Listening: Pay close attention to what the client is saying and clarify points by summarizing their statements. This not only ensures understanding but also shows the client that you are engaged and value their input.

Gathering Information

1. Data Collection: Collect data on current processes, performance metrics, and customer feedback. This data will help you identify areas where generative AI can add value.

2. Stakeholder Interviews: Conduct in-depth interviews with stakeholders from different departments to gain diverse perspectives on the organization's needs and challenges.

3. Surveys and Questionnaires: Distribute surveys or questionnaires to gather quantitative data from a larger group of employees. This can highlight common pain points and areas for improvement.

Analyzing Current Processes

1. Process Mapping: Create visual representations of the organization's current workflows and processes. This helps identify inefficiencies and potential areas for automation or enhancement through generative AI.

2. SWOT Analysis: Conduct a SWOT analysis (Strengths, Weaknesses, Opportunities, Threats) to understand the internal and external factors affecting the organization. This can help pinpoint areas where AI could provide a competitive advantage.

3. Gap Analysis: Compare the current state of the organization's processes with their desired future state. Identify the gaps that generative AI can help bridge, focusing on improving efficiency, accuracy, and innovation.

Identifying Opportunities for Generative AI

Once you have a clear understanding of the client's needs, the next step is to identify specific opportunities where generative AI can be applied effectively.

Reviewing Industry Trends

1. Market Research: Stay updated on the latest trends and developments in generative AI. This includes advancements in technology, emerging applications, and successful case studies from various industries.
2. Competitor Analysis: Analyze how competitors in the client's industry are using generative AI. Identify best practices and potential areas where your client can gain a competitive edge.
3. Regulatory Environment: Understand the regulatory landscape and how it might impact the use of generative AI in the client's industry. Ensure that any proposed solutions comply with relevant laws and regulations.

Brainstorming Sessions

1. Collaborative Workshops: Organize workshops with client stakeholders to brainstorm potential applications of generative AI. Encourage creative thinking and out-of-the-box ideas.
2. Idea Prioritization: Evaluate the feasibility and potential impact of each idea. Use criteria such as alignment with business goals, ease of implementation, and expected ROI to prioritize the most promising opportunities.
3. Proof of Concept (PoC): Select a few high-potential ideas to develop into PoCs. This allows you to test the viability of the solutions in a controlled environment before full-scale implementation.

Use Cases and Examples

1. Personalized Marketing: Use generative AI to create personalized marketing content, such as email campaigns, social media posts, and advertisements, tailored to individual customer preferences and behaviors.
2. Product Design: Apply generative AI in product design to generate innovative prototypes and optimize existing designs based on user feedback and performance data.
3. Customer Support: Develop AI-driven chatbots and virtual assistants to handle customer inquiries, provide support, and enhance the overall customer experience.
4. Content Creation: Utilize generative AI for content creation in industries such as media, publishing, and entertainment. This includes generating articles, scripts, and even music compositions.

Communicating Findings and Recommendations

Effectively communicating your findings and recommendations to the client is crucial for gaining their buy-in and moving forward with your proposed solutions.

Creating Comprehensive Reports

1. Executive Summary: Provide a concise overview of your findings, highlighting the key insights and recommendations. This should be tailored to the client's senior management.
2. Detailed Analysis: Include detailed analysis and supporting data for each identified opportunity. Use visual aids such as charts, graphs, and process maps to enhance clarity.
3. Actionable Recommendations: Offer clear, actionable recommendations for implementing generative AI solutions. Outline the expected benefits, required resources, and potential risks for each recommendation.

Presenting to Stakeholders

1. Engaging Presentations: Create engaging presentations that effectively communicate your findings and recommendations. Use visuals, storytelling, and real-world examples to make your points compelling.
2. Addressing Concerns: Be prepared to address any concerns or objections from stakeholders. Provide evidence-based responses and highlight the potential ROI and strategic benefits of your proposed solutions.
3. Next Steps: Outline the next steps for moving forward with the implementation of generative AI solutions. This includes timelines, milestones, and key deliverables.

Actionable Insights and Examples

To ensure you can effectively identify client needs and opportunities, here are some actionable insights and examples:

Example: Conducting a Needs Assessment

Imagine you are consulting for a healthcare provider looking to improve patient care and operational efficiency. Here's how you might approach the needs assessment:

1. Initial Consultations: Meet with the CEO, medical staff, and administrative personnel to understand their goals and challenges. Key questions might include:

   o "What are your main objectives for improving patient care?"

   o "What administrative processes consume the most time and resources?"

   o "How do you currently gather and use patient data?"

2. Data Collection: Gather data on patient wait times, treatment outcomes, and administrative workflows. Analyze this data to identify bottlenecks and areas for improvement.

3. Stakeholder Interviews: Conduct interviews with doctors, nurses, and administrative staff to gain insights into their daily challenges and pain points.

4. Actionable Insight: Identifying Opportunities for Generative AI
5. To identify opportunities for generative AI, follow these steps:

6. Review Industry Trends: Stay informed about how generative AI is transforming healthcare, such as AI-driven diagnostics, personalized treatment plans, and automated administrative tasks.

7. Brainstorming Sessions: Organize a workshop with healthcare providers to brainstorm potential AI applications. Prioritize ideas such as:

   o Using AI to analyze patient data and suggest personalized treatment plans.

   o Developing a chatbot to handle routine patient inquiries and appointment scheduling.

   o Automating administrative tasks such as billing and patient record management.

8. Proof of Concept: Develop a PoC for an AI-driven diagnostic tool that analyzes medical images to assist doctors in identifying conditions. Test the PoC in a small-scale pilot to evaluate its effectiveness and gather feedback from medical staff.

By conducting thorough needs assessments and identifying high-impact opportunities, you can provide valuable insights and recommendations that drive successful generative AI implementations for your clients. This process not only helps in delivering tailored solutions but also builds trust and credibility with your clients, setting the stage for long-term consulting relationships.

Chapter 5

Crafting Tailored AI Solutions Using GPT Tools

This chapter provides a comprehensive guide to crafting tailored AI solutions using GPT tools, from defining the problem and selecting the right tools to developing, implementing, and integrating AI models. By leveraging GPT tools, you can enhance your consulting practice, deliver more effective solutions, and position yourself as a leading expert in the field.

As a seasoned industry-specific consultant, your expertise is invaluable in identifying opportunities and designing effective solutions. By integrating a chat-GPT-like tool into your practice, you can enhance your capabilities, streamline processes, and deliver more personalized and impactful solutions for your clients.

Designing Custom AI Solutions with GPT

Integrating a chat-GPT tool into the design process can significantly enhance your ability to define problems, select tools, and create detailed solution designs. Here's how to effectively leverage GPT in each stage of the design process.

Defining the Problem Statement

1. Leveraging GPT for Initial Consultations:

    o   Use GPT to facilitate initial discussions with clients, gathering detailed insights through interactive conversations.
    o   GPT can help by generating templates with structured interview questions and summarizing responses, ensuring comprehensive understanding of client needs.

27

2. Refining Objectives with GPT:

   o After initial consultations, use GPT to analyze the gathered data and help refine the project's objectives. GPT can identify key themes and pain points from client interactions.

   o Generate draft problem statements and project scopes with GPT's assistance, ensuring clarity and alignment with client goals.

3. Establishing Success Metrics:

   o GPT can suggest relevant success metrics based on industry standards and project specifics. Use it to draft a list of KPIs and refine them in collaboration with the client.

Selecting the Right AI Tools and Technologies

1. Evaluating AI Technologies:

   o GPT can provide overviews and comparisons of various AI tools and technologies, helping you select the most suitable ones for the project.

   o Use GPT to stay updated on the latest advancements in AI, ensuring your solutions leverage cutting-edge technology.

2. Platform and Infrastructure Recommendations:

   o Leverage GPT to assess the pros and cons of different AI platforms and infrastructure options. It can generate reports based on current industry practices and client-specific requirements.

   o GPT can assist in drafting technical documentation and proposals for chosen platforms, enhancing client communication and approval processes.

3. Ensuring Scalability and Flexibility:

   o GPT can simulate future scenarios and predict scalability issues, helping you choose flexible tools that can grow with the client's needs.

Creating Detailed Solution Designs

1. Solution Architecture Design:

- o Use GPT to draft initial solution architectures, incorporating best practices and innovative design patterns. GPT can help visualize complex systems through diagrams and detailed descriptions.
- o Generate multiple architecture options with GPT and evaluate them collaboratively with your team and client.

2. Data Requirements Identification:

- o GPT can assist in identifying and specifying data requirements, suggesting data sources, and detailing preprocessing steps.
- o Use GPT to create data flow diagrams and documentation, ensuring all stakeholders have a clear understanding of data needs.

3. Workflow Integration Planning:

- o Leverage GPT to draft detailed workflow integration plans. It can help map out processes, identify integration points, and create user interaction models.
- o Use GPT to simulate workflow scenarios, identifying potential bottlenecks and optimization opportunities.

Developing AI Models with GPT

Developing AI models involves data preparation, model training, and evaluation. GPT tools can enhance each of these steps by providing insights, generating code, and facilitating collaboration.

Data Preparation

1. Data Collection and Cleaning:

- o GPT can assist in drafting scripts and code for data collection and cleaning. It can also provide guidelines for ensuring data quality and consistency.
- o Use GPT to generate reports on data quality issues and suggest solutions for common data problems.

2. Data Labeling and Annotation:

- o Leverage GPT to automate parts of the data labeling and annotation process. GPT can suggest labels, validate annotations, and even perform initial labeling for large datasets.

29

o   Use GPT to create guidelines and best practices for data labeling, ensuring accuracy and consistency.

3.   Data Augmentation:

o   GPT can suggest and implement data augmentation techniques, enhancing the training dataset with synthetic examples to improve model robustness.

Model Selection and Training

1.   Choosing Algorithms:

o   GPT can provide recommendations on suitable algorithms based on the problem type and data characteristics. It can generate comparison reports and suggest best practices for algorithm selection.

o   Use GPT to draft detailed descriptions of chosen algorithms and their applicability to the project.

2.   Training Models:

o   Leverage GPT to write training scripts and optimize hyperparameters. GPT can suggest training strategies, monitor progress, and identify potential issues.

o   Use GPT to generate visualizations and reports on model training performance, facilitating collaborative evaluation and decision-making.

3.   Iterative Improvement:

o   GPT can assist in setting up iterative training cycles, suggesting improvements based on performance metrics and feedback.

o   Use GPT to document changes and track improvements across iterations, ensuring a transparent and systematic development process.

Model Evaluation and Validation

1.   Performance Metrics Analysis:

- GPT can help define and calculate relevant performance metrics. It can generate detailed evaluation reports and visualizations, aiding in model assessment.

  - Use GPT to benchmark model performance against industry standards and previous solutions, providing context for evaluation.

2. Real-World Data Testing:

- Leverage GPT to set up testing environments and simulate real-world data scenarios. GPT can help identify potential issues and suggest solutions.
- Use GPT to generate detailed reports on model performance in real-world conditions, facilitating client discussions and decision-making.

3. Bias and Fairness Assessment:

- GPT can assist in identifying and mitigating biases in the model. It can suggest fairness metrics and provide guidelines for ensuring ethical AI practices.
- Use GPT to draft comprehensive bias and fairness reports, ensuring transparency and accountability in the AI solution.

Implementing and Integrating AI Solutions with GPT

Implementing and integrating the AI solution involves deploying the models, integrating them with workflows, and ensuring smooth operation. GPT tools can streamline these processes through automation and enhanced collaboration.

Deployment Strategies

1. Pilot Deployment:

- Use GPT to plan and execute pilot deployments. GPT can generate deployment scripts, monitor performance, and gather feedback for iterative improvements.
- Leverage GPT to document pilot results and prepare reports for client review.

2. CI/CD Implementation:

   o GPT can assist in setting up CI/CD pipelines, automating the deployment process, and ensuring efficient updates and improvements.
   o Use GPT to generate documentation and guidelines for CI/CD practices, facilitating team collaboration and client understanding.

3. Monitoring and Maintenance:

   o Leverage GPT to set up monitoring systems and alert mechanisms. GPT can help track performance metrics, identify issues, and suggest maintenance routines.
   o Use GPT to generate maintenance schedules and documentation, ensuring ongoing solution effectiveness and reliability.

Workflow Integration

1. Seamless Integration:

   o GPT can generate integration scripts and documentation, ensuring compatibility with existing systems and processes.
   o Use GPT to simulate integration scenarios and identify potential issues before full-scale implementation.

2. User Training and Support:

   o Leverage GPT to create training materials, user manuals, and support documentation. GPT can generate interactive tutorials and FAQs, enhancing user adoption.
   o Use GPT to provide ongoing support through chat-based interfaces, addressing user queries and issues in real-time.

3. Change Management:

   o GPT can assist in developing change management strategies, including communication plans and stakeholder engagement. It can generate templates for announcements, training sessions, and feedback collection.
   o Use GPT to monitor and analyze user feedback, continuously improving the AI solution and supporting organizational change.

Actionable Insights and Examples with GPT

To ensure your AI solutions are practical and effective, here are some actionable insights and examples of leveraging GPT in the process:

Example: Designing a Custom AI Solution with GPT

Imagine you are designing a generative AI solution for a retail company to enhance their customer service through personalized product recommendations. Here's how you might approach the design with GPT:

1.   Defining the Problem Statement:

   - Use GPT to facilitate initial consultations and gather insights from client stakeholders. GPT can help draft detailed problem statements and project scopes, ensuring alignment with business goals.

2.   Selecting AI Tools:

   - Leverage GPT to compare and select recommendation engine frameworks. GPT can generate reports on the pros and cons of different frameworks, assisting in the decision-making process.

3.   Creating Detailed Designs:

   - Use GPT to draft comprehensive solution architectures, including data pipelines and integration points. GPT can generate visualizations and documentation to aid client understanding and approval.

Actionable Insight: Developing and Implementing AI Models with GPT

To develop and implement AI models effectively, follow these steps:

1.   Data Preparation:

   - Use GPT to write scripts for data collection and cleaning, ensuring high-quality training data. GPT can assist in labeling and augmenting data, enhancing model performance.

2.   Model Selection and Training:

- Leverage GPT to select suitable algorithms and optimize training processes. GPT can generate training scripts, monitor progress, and suggest improvements, ensuring robust model development.

3.   Deployment and Integration:

- Use GPT to automate deployment processes and integrate the recommendation engine with the e-commerce platform. GPT can provide real-time monitoring and support, ensuring seamless operation and continuous improvement.

By following these steps and incorporating practical examples, you can leverage GPT tools to design, develop, and implement tailored AI solutions that meet your clients' specific needs and deliver significant business value.

Chapter 6

Using GPT in the Consulting Process for Generative AI Implementation

By leveraging GPT throughout the consulting process, Generative AI consultants can enhance their efficiency, accuracy, and the overall value provided to clients. This chapter provides detailed steps and examples to help you integrate GPT into each phase of the consulting process, ensuring successful AI implementation and client satisfaction.

Initial Client Consultation

Understanding Client Needs with GPT

The first step in any consulting engagement is understanding the client's needs. GPT can assist in this phase by helping you frame the right questions and analyze the client's responses effectively. For example, you can use GPT to generate a comprehensive questionnaire:

- "Generate a list of questions to understand a client's requirements for implementing AI in their supply chain management."

GPT can also help summarize and interpret the client's answers, providing a clearer picture of their needs and goals:

- "Summarize the key points from the client's responses about their current challenges in data management."

Crafting Proposals and Engagement Letters

Once the client's needs are understood, the next step is to draft a proposal. GPT can assist in creating tailored proposals and engagement letters by providing templates and customization options based on specific client details. For instance:

- "Generate a proposal template for implementing Generative AI in a mid-sized retail business."
- "What should be included in an engagement letter for an AI consultancy?"

Assessment and Analysis

Data Collection and Preprocessing

The assessment phase involves collecting and preprocessing data. GPT can streamline these tasks by suggesting data collection methods, preprocessing techniques, and tools. For example:

- "What are the best data collection methods for customer behavior analysis in e-commerce?"
- "How can I preprocess text data for sentiment analysis using Python?"

Analyzing Client Data with GPT

GPT can assist in analyzing the collected data to identify patterns, trends, and insights. By feeding GPT with the data and specifying the analysis goals, you can obtain valuable insights quickly. For example:

- "Analyze this dataset to identify key factors influencing customer churn in a telecom company."
- "What trends can be identified from this sales data over the past five years?"

Identifying Opportunities for AI Implementation

Based on the analysis, GPT can help identify specific areas where Generative AI can be applied to enhance business processes. For instance:

- "Suggest areas in supply chain management where Generative AI can improve efficiency."
- "What are the potential applications of AI in healthcare data management?"

Developing an AI Strategy

Crafting a Strategic AI Roadmap

Developing a strategic roadmap is crucial for successful AI implementation. GPT can help outline a detailed AI strategy, including short-term and long-term goals, milestones, and resource allocation. For example:

- "Help me create a strategic roadmap for implementing AI in a financial services firm."
- "What milestones should be included in an AI implementation plan for a manufacturing company?"

Aligning AI Strategy with Business Objectives

- Ensuring that the AI strategy aligns with the client's business objectives is critical. GPT can assist in mapping AI initiatives to business goals and KPIs. For instance:
- "How can AI-driven customer insights support business growth in the retail sector?"
- "What KPIs should be tracked to measure the success of AI implementation in marketing?"

Solution Design and Development

Designing AI Solutions with GPT

GPT can aid in designing AI solutions tailored to the client's needs. This includes selecting appropriate algorithms, defining the architecture, and planning the development process. For example:

- "Suggest an AI architecture for real-time fraud detection in online banking."
- "What algorithms are best suited for predictive maintenance in industrial equipment?"

Developing Prototypes and MVPs

Developing prototypes and minimum viable products (MVPs) is a key step in AI implementation. GPT can assist by providing coding examples, suggesting development tools, and offering debugging tips. For instance:

- "Generate a Python script for a basic chatbot using GPT-3."
- "What tools can be used to develop an MVP for an AI-based recommendation system?"

Leveraging GPT in the Development Phase

During the development phase, GPT can be utilized to write and optimize code, troubleshoot issues, and generate documentation. For example:

- "Help me debug this Python code for a neural network."
- "Generate documentation for an AI-powered customer service application."

Implementation and Integration

Implementing AI Solutions with GPT

Implementation involves deploying the developed AI solutions into the client's environment. GPT can assist with deployment strategies, integration techniques, and performance optimization. For example:

- "What are the best practices for deploying AI models in a cloud environment?"
- "How can I integrate an AI-based recommendation engine into an existing e-commerce platform?"

Ensuring Seamless Integration

Seamless integration of AI solutions with existing systems is crucial. GPT can suggest integration approaches and provide guidance on compatibility and interoperability. For instance:

- "How can I integrate an AI chatbot with a CRM system?"
- "What are the common challenges in integrating AI solutions with legacy systems?"

Monitoring and Maintenance

Setting Up Monitoring Systems

Post-implementation, it's essential to monitor the AI solutions to ensure they function as expected. GPT can help set up monitoring systems and suggest key metrics to track. For example:

- "What are the key metrics for monitoring the performance of an AI-based fraud detection system?"
- "How can I set up an alert system for identifying issues in AI model performance?"

Regular Maintenance and Updates

Regular maintenance and updates are necessary to keep AI solutions effective. GPT can provide guidelines for maintenance schedules, updating models, and handling data drift. For instance:

- "How often should AI models be retrained with new data?"
- "What are the best practices for maintaining an AI system in production?"

Leveraging GPT for Continuous Improvement

GPT can assist in the continuous improvement of AI solutions by analyzing performance data and suggesting enhancements. For example:

- "Analyze the performance data of this AI model and suggest improvements."
- "What are the latest advancements in AI that can be integrated into existing solutions?"

Evaluating Success and ROI - Measuring Success with GPT

Measuring the success of AI implementation involves evaluating various metrics and KPIs. GPT can help design evaluation frameworks and generate reports. For example:

- "Create a framework for evaluating the success of an AI-based marketing campaign."
- "Generate a report on the ROI of implementing AI in customer service."

Conducting Post-Implementation Reviews

Post-implementation reviews are crucial for assessing the overall impact of the AI solutions. GPT can assist in conducting these reviews by providing templates and guiding the analysis. For instance:

- "What should be included in a post-implementation review for an AI project?"
- "Help me analyze the outcomes of an AI implementation in logistics."

Providing Client Feedback and Recommendations

Finally, providing clients with feedback and recommendations for future improvements is essential. GPT can help draft detailed feedback reports and suggest next steps. For example:

- "Draft a feedback report for a client on the success of their AI implementation."
- "What recommendations can be made for scaling AI solutions in a growing business?"

Chapter 7

Leveraging GPT for Business Planning for Generative AI Consultants

By leveraging GPT tools for business planning, Generative AI consultants can streamline their processes, make data-driven decisions, and enhance their strategic planning capabilities. This chapter provides actionable insights and examples to help you effectively utilize GPT in various aspects of business planning, ensuring your consulting business is well-prepared for success (Note: these also apply to assisting clients with their business planning as well).

Defining Your Business Goals and Objectives

- Establishing Clear Goals with GPT
- Incorporating GPT into your business planning starts with defining clear goals and objectives. GPT can assist in articulating these goals by generating comprehensive business statements, mission, and vision based on industry best practices and specific inputs you provide. For example, you can prompt GPT with information about your business, such as:
- "Help me create a mission statement for a Generative AI consulting firm focusing on the healthcare industry."
- GPT can then generate various mission statement options, helping you refine and choose the best fit.

Aligning Objectives with Market Trends

GPT's ability to analyze vast amounts of data can help you align your objectives with current market trends. By feeding GPT information about industry reports, market analyses, and competitor strategies, you can generate insights and forecasts to ensure your goals are realistic and achievable. For example:

- "Generate a summary of current trends in AI consulting within the financial sector."
- "Based on these trends, what should be the primary objectives for a startup AI consultancy?"

Setting KPIs with GPT

Establishing key performance indicators (KPIs) is crucial for tracking progress. GPT can help identify relevant KPIs based on industry standards and specific business goals. You can ask GPT to suggest KPIs for different aspects of your business, such as:

- "What KPIs should I track for client acquisition in a Generative AI consulting firm?"
- "How can I measure the success of AI implementation projects?"

Creating a Comprehensive Business Plan

Outlining Business Strategies with GPT

GPT can aid in drafting a comprehensive business plan by providing templates and examples tailored to your needs. You can request detailed outlines or sections of a business plan, such as market analysis, service offerings, and competitive strategy. For example:

- "Generate a market analysis for a Generative AI consulting firm targeting the retail industry."
- "What should be included in the competitive strategy section of a business plan for an AI consultancy?"

Financial Planning and Forecasting

Using GPT for financial planning can streamline the process of creating realistic revenue projections and cost estimations. By inputting financial data and assumptions, GPT can help generate financial models and forecasts. For example:

- "Create a three-year financial projection for an AI consulting startup with an initial investment of $200,000."
- "What are the typical costs associated with starting a Generative AI consultancy?"

Risk Analysis and Mitigation

GPT can also assist in identifying potential risks and developing mitigation strategies. By analyzing industry reports and historical data, GPT can highlight common risks and suggest ways to address them. For example:

- "What are the common risks faced by AI consultants in the healthcare sector?"
- "How can these risks be mitigated effectively?"

Financial Planning and Forecasting for a Generative AI Startup

Understanding Financial Aspects with GPT

Financial planning is a critical component of business success. GPT can help you understand and plan for various financial aspects of your Generative AI consulting business, such as startup costs, operational expenses, and revenue streams. For instance:

- "List the typical startup costs for a Generative AI consultancy."
- "What are the main revenue streams for an AI consulting firm?"

Exploring Funding Options

GPT can provide insights into different funding options available for startups. By analyzing your business model and financial needs, GPT can suggest suitable funding sources and strategies. For example:

- "What are the best funding options for an AI consulting startup focusing on manufacturing?"
- "How can I prepare a compelling pitch for potential investors?"

Financial Management and Sustainability

GPT can assist in developing strategies for sustainable financial management. This includes budgeting, cash flow management, and financial reporting. For example:

- "How should I structure a budget for the first year of my AI consulting business?"
- "What are the best practices for managing cash flow in a consultancy?"

Cost Management Strategies for a Generative AI Startup

Identifying Cost Drivers with GPT

Effective cost management starts with understanding the main cost drivers in your business. GPT can help identify these drivers and suggest optimization strategies. For example:

- "What are the main cost drivers for a Generative AI consultancy?"
- "How can I optimize costs related to cloud computing resources?"

Cost-Saving Techniques

GPT can suggest various cost-saving techniques, such as automating routine tasks, outsourcing non-core activities, and leveraging open-source AI tools. For instance:

- "What are some cost-saving techniques for an AI consulting business?"
- "How can I reduce costs associated with data processing and storage?"

Budgeting and Expense Tracking

Developing a Budget with GPT

Creating a detailed budget is essential for financial planning. GPT can assist in developing budgets by providing templates and guiding you through the process. For example:

- "Help me create a budget template for a Generative AI consultancy."

- "What should be included in the budget for the first year of an AI consulting firm?"

Implementing Expense Tracking Systems

Tracking expenses is crucial for maintaining financial health. GPT can suggest tools and systems for efficient expense tracking and management. For example:

- "What are the best tools for tracking expenses in a consulting business?"
- "How can I set up an expense tracking system for my AI consultancy?"

Financial Record-Keeping and Reporting

Best Practices for Record-Keeping

Maintaining accurate financial records is vital for compliance and decision-making. GPT can provide best practices and guidelines for financial record-keeping. For example:

- "What are the best practices for financial record-keeping in a consulting business?"
- "How can I ensure compliance with financial reporting standards?"

Preparing Financial Statements

GPT can help generate financial statements and reports, ensuring you have a clear understanding of your business's financial health. For instance:

- "Help me prepare a profit and loss statement for my AI consulting firm."
- "What should be included in a financial report for investors?"

Evaluating and Adjusting Pricing Models

Understanding Pricing Models with GPT

GPT can provide insights into different pricing models used in the Generative AI consulting industry, helping you choose the most appropriate one for your business. For example:

- "What are the common pricing models for AI consulting services?"
- "How do I decide between project-based and retainer pricing?"

Adjusting Pricing Strategies

As your business grows, you may need to adjust your pricing strategies. GPT can help analyze market conditions and suggest optimal pricing adjustments. For example:

- "How can I adjust my pricing strategy to remain competitive in the AI consulting market?"
- "What factors should I consider when revising my pricing model?"

Chapter 8

Marketing and Promoting Your Generative AI Services

By leveraging GPT in your marketing and promotion efforts, you can streamline processes, create compelling content, and engage effectively with your audience. This chapter provides detailed steps and examples to help you harness the power of GPT for marketing your generative AI consulting services, ensuring growth and success in a competitive market.

Building a Strong Brand

Establishing Your Unique Value Proposition (UVP) with GPT

Your unique value proposition (UVP) differentiates your services from competitors. GPT can help articulate a compelling UVP by analyzing market trends and identifying gaps in current offerings. For example:

- "Analyze the current market for AI consulting services and identify gaps that our company can fill."
- "Generate a UVP for a consulting firm specializing in generative AI for healthcare."

Crafting a Brand Story

A strong brand story connects emotionally with your audience. GPT can assist in crafting an engaging narrative by generating story ideas and refining your message. For example:

- "Help me create a brand story for a company offering generative AI solutions for small businesses."

- "What elements should be included in a compelling brand narrative for a tech startup?"

Designing a Professional Brand Identity

A consistent brand identity across all platforms builds recognition. GPT can suggest design elements, color schemes, and typography that align with your brand values. For instance:

- "What color schemes and typography are best suited for a high-tech AI consultancy?"
- "Generate a list of design elements that convey innovation and trustworthiness."

Creating a Marketing Strategy with GPT

A well-defined marketing strategy is essential for attracting clients and building your brand in the generative AI consulting industry. Leveraging GPT can help you develop a comprehensive strategy that includes key components such as defining your target audience, articulating your unique value proposition, and identifying the most effective marketing channels. Here's how to do it:

1. Defining Your Target Audience

Understanding your target audience is the first step in creating an effective marketing strategy. This involves identifying the industry segments, company sizes, and decision-makers who are most likely to benefit from your generative AI services. GPT can assist in refining your target audience with data-driven insights.

Industry Segments

Identify the specific industries that can benefit most from generative AI. GPT can analyze market trends and industry reports to highlight sectors with high potential.

Example Prompts:

- "Analyze current market trends and suggest industries that are rapidly adopting generative AI."

- "What industries have the highest demand for AI-driven automation solutions?"

Company Sizes

Determine the size of companies that are ideal clients. GPT can help analyze your past client data to identify patterns in company size and AI adoption.

Example Prompts:

- "Based on our previous projects, what company sizes (in terms of revenue or employees) have shown the most interest in our AI services?"
- "Generate a list of benefits for small businesses implementing generative AI."

Decision-Makers

Identify the key decision-makers within these companies. GPT can provide insights into the roles and responsibilities of potential clients and suggest strategies for reaching them.

Example Prompts:

- "Who are the primary decision-makers for AI technology investments in mid-sized tech companies?"
- "What are the common pain points for CTOs in the healthcare industry that our AI solutions can address?"

2. Articulating Your Unique Value Proposition

Your unique value proposition (UVP) is what sets your services apart from the competition. GPT can help you articulate a clear and compelling UVP that resonates with your target audience.

Addressing Client Needs

GPT can assist in identifying the specific needs and challenges of your target audience, ensuring your UVP addresses these effectively.

Example Prompts:

- "Generate a list of common challenges faced by manufacturing companies that could be solved with generative AI."
- "How can our AI-driven customer service solutions specifically benefit e-commerce businesses?"

Highlighting Unique Offerings

Articulate what makes your services unique, such as proprietary technologies, specialized expertise, or exceptional customer support.

Example Prompts:

- "What are our unique selling points compared to other AI consulting firms?"
- "How can we highlight our proprietary AI algorithms in our value proposition?"

Creating Compelling Messaging

Craft messaging that clearly communicates your UVP in a way that resonates with your audience. GPT can help refine your language to be both persuasive and clear.

Example Prompts:

- "Create a concise and compelling value proposition statement for our AI consulting services."
- "Refine this value proposition to emphasize our quick implementation times and high ROI."

3. Identifying Effective Marketing Channels

Choosing the right marketing channels is crucial for reaching your target audience effectively. GPT can help identify and optimize these channels based on your audience's preferences and behaviors.

Online Advertising

Online advertising, including search engine marketing and social media ads, can be highly effective. GPT can assist in keyword research, ad copy creation, and audience targeting.

Example Prompts:

- "What keywords should we target for a Google Ads campaign promoting our AI services?"
- "Write ad copy for a LinkedIn campaign aimed at decision-makers in the tech industry."

Content Marketing

Content marketing, such as blogs, whitepapers, and webinars, helps establish your expertise and attract organic traffic. GPT can generate content ideas, outlines, and even full drafts.

Example Prompts:

- "Generate blog post ideas on the impact of generative AI in the healthcare industry."
- "Create an outline for a whitepaper on the benefits of AI in financial services."

Networking Events

Attending industry conferences, webinars, and networking events can help you connect with potential clients. GPT can identify relevant events and help prepare presentations or speaking points.

Example Prompts:

- "List upcoming AI conferences that we should consider attending."
- "Generate talking points for a presentation on the future of generative AI in retail."

4. Implementing and Monitoring Your Strategy

Once your strategy is defined, implementing and continuously monitoring its effectiveness is crucial. GPT can help set up tracking mechanisms and provide insights for ongoing optimization.

Setting Up Tracking

Track the performance of your marketing activities to understand what's working and what's not. GPT can suggest key performance indicators (KPIs) and tools for monitoring.

Example Prompts:

- "What KPIs should we track to measure the success of our content marketing efforts?"
- "Recommend tools for tracking the performance of our social media campaigns."

Analyzing Performance

Regularly analyze the data to gain insights and make data-driven adjustments. GPT can help interpret the data and suggest improvements.

Example Prompts:

- "Analyze the performance of our latest email marketing campaign and provide improvement suggestions."
- "What changes can we make to our online advertising strategy to improve ROI?"

Continuous Improvement

Marketing is an iterative process. Use insights gained from data analysis to continuously refine and improve your strategy. GPT can help brainstorm new ideas and approaches.

Example Prompts:

- "Suggest new content topics based on the performance of our previous blog posts."
- "How can we optimize our email marketing strategy for better engagement?"

By leveraging GPT in creating and refining your marketing strategy, you can ensure that your generative AI consulting services are effectively promoted to the right audience, with compelling messaging and through the most effective channels. This comprehensive approach will help you build a strong brand, attract new clients, and drive business growth.

Creating High-Quality Content - Developing a Content Strategy with GPT

A robust content strategy is essential for attracting and retaining clients. GPT can help you develop a content calendar, suggest topics, and optimize content for SEO. For example:

- "Create a content calendar for a blog focused on generative AI applications."
- "What are the trending topics in AI that we should cover in our blog?"

Writing Engaging Blog Posts

GPT can generate ideas for blog posts, provide outlines, and even draft content. This can save time and ensure your content is informative and engaging. For instance:

- "Generate blog post ideas on the impact of generative AI in the finance industry."
- "Write an outline for a blog post on how AI can enhance customer service."

Crafting Compelling Case Studies and Whitepapers

Case studies and whitepapers demonstrate your expertise and success stories. GPT can help structure these documents and provide content that highlights key achievements. For example:

- "Outline a case study on our recent AI implementation project for a retail client."
- "Generate content for a whitepaper on the future of generative AI in manufacturing."

Leveraging Social Media and Online Presence

Optimizing Social Media Profiles with GPT

Your social media profiles are often the first point of contact with potential clients. GPT can suggest profile updates, post ideas, and engagement strategies. For example:

- "What should our LinkedIn profile highlight to attract AI consulting clients?"
- "Generate a list of social media post ideas for promoting generative AI services."

Creating Shareable Content

Creating content that resonates with your audience is crucial for social media success. GPT can help generate engaging posts, infographics, and videos. For instance:

- "Write a LinkedIn post about the benefits of generative AI for small businesses."
- "What are some infographic ideas that explain the uses of AI in healthcare?"

Engaging with Your Audience

Active engagement with your audience builds trust and fosters relationships. GPT can suggest responses to comments, questions, and direct messages. For example:

- "How should we respond to a client inquiry about our AI services on Twitter?"
- "Generate a reply to a positive review on our Facebook page."

Email Marketing Campaigns

Building an Email List

Building a targeted email list is essential for effective email marketing. GPT can suggest strategies for growing your list and segmenting your audience. For instance:

- "What are some strategies for building an email list for an AI consultancy?"
- "How can we segment our email list based on client interests and needs?"

Crafting Effective Email Campaigns

GPT can help you craft personalized and engaging email campaigns that convert. This includes writing subject lines, body content, and CTAs. For example:

- "Generate subject lines for an email campaign promoting our new AI service offerings."
- "Write an email template for re-engaging past clients with a special offer."

Automating Email Workflows

Automating email workflows ensures timely and relevant communication with your audience. GPT can assist in setting up automation sequences and writing content for each step. For instance:

- "What email sequences should we set up for new subscribers to our AI newsletter?"
- "Write the content for a welcome email series for new clients."

Networking and Partnerships

Identifying Networking Opportunities with GPT

Networking is crucial for business growth. GPT can help identify relevant industry events, conferences, and meetups where you can connect with potential clients and partners. For example:

- "What are the top AI conferences to attend this year?"
- "Generate a list of local business meetups focused on technology and innovation."

Crafting Elevator Pitches

An effective elevator pitch can open doors to new opportunities. GPT can help refine your pitch to make it concise, engaging, and memorable. For instance:

- "Help me craft an elevator pitch for our generative AI consulting services."
- "What are key elements to include in an elevator pitch for tech startups?"

Building Strategic Partnerships

Building partnerships can expand your reach and capabilities. GPT can suggest potential partners and provide templates for partnership proposals. For example:

- "What companies should we consider partnering with to enhance our AI services?"
- "Generate a template for a partnership proposal with a technology provider."

Utilizing Paid Advertising

Planning Advertising Campaigns with GPT

Paid advertising can drive targeted traffic to your services. GPT can help plan campaigns, identify keywords, and set budgets. For example:

- "What keywords should we target for a Google Ads campaign promoting AI consulting services?"
- "How should we allocate our budget for a LinkedIn advertising campaign?"

Creating Ad Copy and Visuals

GPT can assist in writing compelling ad copy and suggesting visuals that capture attention. For instance:

- "Write a Facebook ad copy for our new AI-driven customer service solution."
- "What visuals should accompany an ad promoting our generative AI services?"

Tracking and Optimizing Campaign Performance

Monitoring and optimizing your campaigns ensures maximum ROI. GPT can suggest metrics to track and provide insights for improving performance. For example:

- "What metrics should we track to measure the success of our PPC campaign?"

- "Generate a report on the performance of our recent social media ad campaign."

Leveraging GPT for Continuous Improvement

Analyzing Marketing Data

Continuous improvement requires analyzing marketing data to identify what works and what doesn't. GPT can help analyze this data and provide actionable insights. For instance:

- "Analyze our website traffic data and suggest improvements for increasing conversions."
- "What are the key takeaways from our latest email marketing campaign?"

Staying Updated with Industry Trends

The AI industry is constantly evolving and staying updated with trends is crucial. GPT can help you stay informed by summarizing industry reports, news, and research papers. For example:

- "Summarize the latest trends in generative AI from this industry report."
- "What are the recent advancements in AI that we should be aware of?"

Incorporating Client Feedback

Client feedback is invaluable for improving your services. GPT can help analyze feedback and suggest areas for enhancement. For instance:

- "Analyze client feedback from our latest project and provide improvement suggestions."
- "How can we use client testimonials to enhance our marketing efforts?"

Chapter 9

Working Efficiently and Prioritizing Projects

Effective time management and project prioritization are essential skills for generative AI consultants. Leveraging GPT can enhance these processes by providing valuable insights and tools for managing time, projects, and collaboration effectively.

Time Management Strategies

Effective time management is crucial for handling multiple projects and maintaining productivity. Strategies include:

Prioritization

Prioritize tasks based on their urgency and importance, using frameworks like the Eisenhower Matrix. GPT can help analyze tasks and categorize them appropriately.

Example:

- o Eisenhower Matrix Creation: Ask GPT to create an Eisenhower Matrix for your weekly tasks. *Prompt*: "Create an Eisenhower Matrix for the following tasks: finalize client proposal, attend industry webinar, review project deliverables, update company website, and respond to client emails." *Response*: GPT generates a matrix categorizing tasks into urgent/important, not urgent/important, urgent/not important, and not urgent/not important.

Time Blocking

Use time blocking to allocate specific periods for focused work, meetings, and administrative tasks. GPT can assist in creating an optimal schedule.

Example:

o   Daily Routine Optimization: Use GPT to suggest a daily schedule that includes time blocks for different activities. *Prompt*: "Create a daily schedule with time blocks for client work, business development, professional development, and administrative tasks, ensuring a balanced workload." *Response*: GPT provides a detailed schedule, e.g., 9-11 AM: Client Work, 11-12 PM: Business Development, 1-3 PM: Professional Development, 3-5 PM: Administrative Tasks.

Productivity Tools

Utilize productivity tools, such as task management apps and calendars, to stay organized and on track. GPT can recommend and help set up these tools.

Example:

o   Tool Recommendation: Ask GPT to recommend productivity tools based on specific needs. *Prompt*: "Recommend productivity tools for task management, time tracking, and calendar organization for a generative AI consultant." *Response*: GPT suggests tools like Trello for task management, Toggl for time tracking, and Google Calendar for scheduling.

Implementing a Routine Example:

o   Implement a daily routine that includes dedicated time blocks for client work, business development, and professional development to ensure you balance all aspects of your consulting practice. *Prompt*: "Create a weekly routine with balanced time blocks for client work, business development, and professional development." *Response*: GPT generates a routine such as:
    o   Monday: 9-12 Client Work, 1-3 Business Development, 3-5 Professional Development
    o   Tuesday: 9-12 Client Work, 1-5 Client Meetings
    o   And so on...

Project Management Techniques

Effective project management ensures successful project delivery and client satisfaction. Techniques include:

Project Planning

Develop detailed project plans that outline objectives, deliverables, timelines, and resources. GPT can help draft comprehensive project plans.

Example:

- o Project Plan Creation: Use GPT to develop a detailed project plan. *Prompt:* "Create a project plan for developing a generative AI solution for an e-commerce client, including objectives, deliverables, timelines, and required resources." *Response:* GPT provides a detailed project plan, including phases like requirement gathering, solution design, development, testing, and deployment with timelines and resource allocation.

Agile Methodology

Use agile methodologies, such as Scrum or Kanban, to manage projects in iterative cycles and adapt to changes. GPT can assist in setting up agile processes and sprints.

Example:

- o Agile Sprint Planning: Ask GPT to help plan agile sprints. *Prompt:* "Plan the first sprint for a generative AI project using Scrum methodology, including tasks, timelines, and goals." *Response:* GPT generates a sprint plan, e.g., Sprint 1: Task breakdown, timeline for two weeks, goals like completing the initial prototype, and review meeting schedules.

Collaboration Tools

Use collaboration tools, such as Trello, Asana, or Jira, to manage tasks, track progress, and facilitate communication with clients and team members. GPT can recommend and assist in setting up these tools.

Example:

○ Tool Setup: Use GPT to set up a project in a collaboration tool. *Prompt*: "Set up a new project in Asana for managing a generative AI implementation, including task breakdown, deadlines, and team assignments." *Response*: GPT outlines the setup process, creating tasks, assigning deadlines, and adding team members.

Actionable Insight:

○ Conduct regular project reviews to assess progress, identify any issues, and make necessary adjustments to stay on track. *Prompt*: "Provide a structure for conducting regular project reviews and reporting progress to stakeholders." *Response*: GPT suggests a structure including progress updates, milestone achievements, issue identification, and action items for the next period.

Collaborating with Clients and Teams

Effective collaboration with clients and team members is key to successful project outcomes. Consider the following:

Clear Communication

Establish clear communication channels and protocols to ensure everyone is on the same page. GPT can draft communication plans and protocols.

Example:

○ Communication Plan: Use GPT to create a communication plan. *Prompt*: "Draft a communication plan for a generative AI project, including channels, frequency, and key points of contact." *Response*: GPT provides a detailed plan, specifying email, Slack, and video calls as channels, weekly updates, and main contacts for each phase of the project.

Regular Updates

Provide regular updates to clients and stakeholders on project progress, milestones, and any potential issues. GPT can help draft update reports and presentations.

Example:

- o Update Reports: Use GPT to generate regular project updates. *Prompt*: "Draft a bi-weekly project update report for a client, summarizing progress, milestones achieved, and any issues." *Response*: GPT creates a template for bi-weekly updates, including sections for progress summary, milestone achievements, issues, and next steps.

Feedback and Iteration

Encourage feedback from clients and team members and iterate on your solutions based on their input. GPT can facilitate feedback collection and iteration planning.

Example:

- o Feedback Collection: Use GPT to design feedback forms and process. *Prompt*: "Create a feedback form for clients to provide input on our generative AI solution, and outline a process for incorporating feedback." *Response*: GPT designs a feedback form with questions on solution effectiveness, user experience, and suggestions for improvement, along with a process for reviewing and implementing feedback.

Example:

- o Schedule regular check-in meetings with clients to discuss progress, address any concerns, and ensure alignment with project goals. *Prompt*: "Outline a structure for regular client check-in meetings, including agenda items and follow-up actions." *Response*: GPT suggests a meeting structure with agenda items like progress updates, issue discussion, milestone review, and follow-up action items.

By leveraging GPT in developing and implementing time management strategies, project management techniques, and collaboration practices, generative AI consultants can work more efficiently and effectively, ensuring successful project outcomes and high client satisfaction.

Chapter 10

Scaling and Growing Your Generative AI Business

Scaling your generative AI consulting business involves expanding your services, client base, and team. Leveraging GPT can enhance these processes by providing valuable insights and tools for business development, team building, and sustainable growth.

Strategies for Scaling Your Business

Scaling your consulting practice involves expanding your services, client base, and team. Strategies include:

Service Expansion

Expand your service offerings to include new areas, such as AI training, advisory services, or managed AI solutions. GPT can help identify trends and potential new services that align with your expertise and market demand.

Example:

o   Service Expansion Analysis: Use GPT to analyze industry trends and suggest new service offerings. *Prompt:* "Analyze the current trends in the AI consulting market and suggest new service areas we could expand into, such as AI training, advisory services, or managed AI solutions." *Response:* GPT provides a detailed analysis highlighting growing demand for AI ethics training, AI governance advisory services, and end-to-end AI deployment solutions, including practical steps to develop these services.

Geographic Expansion

Explore opportunities to expand into new geographic markets, either domestically or internationally. GPT can help perform market analysis and identify high-potential regions.

Example:

- o Geographic Market Analysis: Use GPT to conduct market research on potential expansion regions. *Prompt:* "Perform a market analysis to identify high-potential geographic regions for expanding our AI consulting services, considering factors like market demand, competition, and regulatory environment." *Response:* GPT generates a comprehensive report identifying regions like North America, Europe, and Southeast Asia, detailing market size, growth potential, competitive landscape, and regulatory considerations.

Partnerships and Alliances

Form strategic partnerships and alliances with other firms to leverage complementary skills and resources. GPT can help identify potential partners and draft partnership proposals.

Example:

- o Identifying Partners: Use GPT to identify potential strategic partners. *Prompt:* "Identify potential strategic partners in the AI industry that complement our services and could help us scale our business." *Response:* GPT lists companies specializing in AI hardware, cloud services, or specific AI applications and suggests collaboration opportunities, such as joint ventures or referral agreements.

Actionable Insight:

- o Conduct a market analysis to identify high-potential areas for expansion and develop a strategic plan for entering these markets. *Prompt:* "Create a strategic plan for expanding into high-potential areas identified through market analysis, including service offerings, target clients, and entry strategies." *Response:* GPT provides a strategic plan outline, including steps for market entry, marketing strategies, and initial service offerings tailored to the new market.

Hiring and Building a Team

Building a strong team is essential for scaling your business and delivering high-quality services. Consider the following:

Talent Acquisition

Develop a talent acquisition strategy to attract and hire top talent with the skills and experience needed for your business. GPT can assist in drafting job descriptions and sourcing candidates.

Example:

- o Job Descriptions and Sourcing: Use GPT to draft job descriptions and identify potential hiring channels. *Prompt*: "Draft job descriptions for data scientists, machine learning engineers, and AI ethicists, and suggest the best channels for sourcing top talent." *Response*: GPT generates detailed job descriptions for each role and recommends sourcing channels like LinkedIn, specialized job boards, and university partnerships.

Team Development

Invest in training and development programs to upskill your team and keep them abreast of the latest AI advancements. GPT can suggest relevant training programs and resources.

Example:

- o Training Program Suggestions: Use GPT to recommend training programs and certifications. *Prompt*: "Suggest training programs and certifications to upskill our AI consulting team, focusing on the latest advancements in AI and machine learning." *Response*: GPT provides a list of reputable training programs, such as courses from Coursera, edX, and Udacity, and certifications like TensorFlow Developer Certificate and AWS Certified Machine Learning.

Culture and Leadership

Foster a positive company culture and provide strong leadership to motivate and retain your team. GPT can help draft policies and initiatives that promote a healthy work environment.

Example:

o Culture and Leadership Initiatives: Use GPT to develop initiatives for fostering a positive company culture. *Prompt*: "Develop initiatives and policies to foster a positive company culture and strong leadership within our generative AI consulting team." *Response*: GPT suggests initiatives such as regular team-building activities, transparent communication policies, leadership training programs, and employee recognition programs.

Example:

o Hire specialists in different areas of AI, such as data scientists, machine learning engineers, and AI ethicists, to enhance your service offerings and expertise. *Prompt*: "Outline a hiring plan to attract and onboard specialists in data science, machine learning engineering, and AI ethics." *Response*: GPT provides a detailed hiring plan, including steps for job posting, candidate evaluation, interview processes, and onboarding procedures.

Ensuring Sustainable Growth

Sustainable growth involves balancing expansion with maintaining quality and profitability. Strategies include:

Process Optimization

Optimizing your business processes will help improve efficiency and reduce costs. GPT can analyze existing processes and suggest improvements.

Example:

o Process Improvement: Use GPT to identify inefficiencies in current business processes and suggest optimizations. *Prompt*: "Analyze our current project management and client onboarding processes and suggest improvements to enhance efficiency and reduce costs." *Response*: GPT provides a detailed analysis identifying bottlenecks and inefficiencies, with suggestions like automating client onboarding, streamlining communication channels, and adopting lean project management practices.

Quality Control

Implement quality control measures to ensure consistent delivery of high-quality services. GPT can help develop quality control frameworks and checklists.

Example:

- o Quality Control Framework: Use GPT to create a quality control framework for your consulting services. *Prompt:* "Develop a quality control framework to ensure the consistent delivery of high-quality generative AI consulting services." *Response:* GPT outlines a framework including quality assurance processes, client feedback loops, and regular internal audits to maintain service standards.

Financial Management

Monitor your financial performance and make data-driven decisions to ensure profitability and sustainability. GPT can assist in financial analysis and forecasting.

Example:

- o Financial Analysis and Forecasting: Use GPT to perform financial analysis and create forecasts. *Prompt:* "Perform a financial analysis of our current consulting operations and create a forecast for the next fiscal year." *Response:* GPT provides a financial analysis including revenue, expenses, and profit margins, along with a forecast predicting future financial performance based on different growth scenarios.

Actionable Insight:

- o Regularly review your business processes and performance metrics to identify areas for improvement and ensure sustainable growth. *Prompt:* "Create a template for regular reviews of business processes and performance metrics to identify areas for improvement." *Response:* GPT generates a review template that includes key performance indicators (KPIs), areas to assess (e.g., client satisfaction, project efficiency), and a process for implementing improvements.

By leveraging GPT in developing strategies for scaling, hiring, and ensuring sustainable growth, generative AI consultants can efficiently expand their businesses while maintaining high-quality service delivery and profitability.

Chapter 11

Managing Business Risk and Ensuring Maximum Profitability

Managing business risk and maximizing profitability are critical for the success of your generative AI consulting practice. Leveraging GPT can enhance your ability to identify risks, implement effective mitigation strategies, ensure data privacy and security, optimize revenue streams, control costs, and maintain financial compliance.

Risk Management Strategies

Effective risk management helps protect your business from potential threats and uncertainties. Strategies include:

Risk Identification

Identify potential risks such as market fluctuations, regulatory changes, and technological disruptions. GPT can assist in conducting comprehensive risk assessments.

Example:

o Comprehensive Risk Assessment: Use GPT to conduct a comprehensive risk assessment. *Prompt*: "Identify potential risks to our generative AI consulting business, considering market trends, regulatory environments, and technological changes." *Response*: GPT provides a detailed risk register including market volatility risks, regulatory compliance risks (e.g., GDPR, CCPA), and emerging technology risks (e.g., AI advancements affecting service relevance).

Risk Mitigation

Develop and implement risk mitigation plans to reduce the impact of identified risks. GPT can suggest mitigation strategies based on industry best practices.

Example:

- o Risk Mitigation Strategy: Use GPT to develop a risk mitigation plan for identified risks. *Prompt:* "Develop a risk mitigation plan to address identified risks such as market fluctuations and regulatory changes." *Response:* GPT outlines strategies such as diversifying service offerings, monitoring regulatory updates, and establishing contingency plans for disruptive technologies.

Insurance

Obtain appropriate insurance coverage to protect your business from liability, cyber threats, and other risks. GPT can recommend suitable insurance options based on your business profile.

Example:

- o Insurance Coverage Analysis: Use GPT to analyze insurance coverage options. *Prompt:* "Evaluate insurance coverage options to protect our generative AI consulting business from liability and cyber threats." *Response:* GPT provides a comparison of insurance policies including general liability, cyber liability, and professional indemnity, highlighting coverage benefits and costs.

Actionable Insight:

- o Conduct regular risk assessments to identify new risks and update your mitigation plans accordingly, ensuring you are prepared for potential challenges. *Prompt:* "Create a schedule for regular risk assessments and updates to our risk mitigation plans." *Response:* GPT generates a schedule outlining quarterly risk assessment reviews and updates, incorporating feedback loops from stakeholders and industry experts.

Data Privacy and Security

Ensuring data privacy and security is critical in AI consulting, given the sensitivity of client data and the regulatory landscape. Consider the following:

Compliance

Ensure compliance with data privacy regulations such as GDPR, CCPA, and HIPAA, as applicable. GPT can provide guidance on regulatory requirements and compliance measures.

Example:

o   Regulatory Compliance Checklist: Use GPT to create a data privacy compliance checklist. *Prompt:* "Develop a checklist to ensure compliance with GDPR, CCPA, and HIPAA regulations in our AI consulting projects." *Response:* GPT generates a checklist covering data handling practices, consent management, and data breach notification procedures according to regulatory standards.

Security Measures

Implement robust security measures including encryption, access controls, and regular security audits. GPT can recommend cybersecurity best practices tailored to your consulting business.

Example:

o   Cybersecurity Best Practices: Use GPT to outline cybersecurity best practices. *Prompt:* "Implement cybersecurity best practices to protect client data in our generative AI consulting projects." *Response:* GPT provides recommendations such as multi-factor authentication, data encryption protocols, and regular vulnerability assessments to enhance data security.

Client Education

Educate your clients on data privacy and security best practices to ensure they are also taking appropriate measures. GPT can develop client education materials and communication strategies.

Example:

- o Client Education Module: Use GPT to create a client education module on data privacy and security. *Prompt*: "Develop an educational module for clients on best practices for data privacy and security in AI consulting engagements." *Response*: GPT generates an interactive module covering topics like data protection principles, secure data handling procedures, and client responsibilities in maintaining data security.

Actionable Insight:

- o Develop a comprehensive data privacy and security policy and regularly review and update it to reflect the latest best practices and regulatory requirements. *Prompt*: "Update our data privacy and security policy to align with current best practices and regulatory changes." *Response*: GPT provides a revised policy document incorporating updated data handling protocols, legal compliance guidelines, and incident response procedures.

Maximizing Profitability

Maximizing profitability involves optimizing your revenue streams and controlling costs. Strategies include:

Value-Based Pricing

Implement value-based pricing models that reflect the value you deliver to clients, rather than just the time spent. GPT can assist in analyzing client value propositions and pricing strategies.

Example:

- o Value-Based Pricing Analysis: Use GPT to analyze value-based pricing strategies. *Prompt*: "Develop a value-based pricing model for our AI consulting services that reflects the unique value we deliver to clients." *Response*: GPT provides a pricing model incorporating factors like project complexity, client ROI, and market competitiveness to optimize pricing structures.

Upselling and Cross-Selling

72

Identify opportunities to upsell and cross-sell additional services to existing clients. GPT can analyze client data and recommend personalized service offerings.

Example:

o Client Engagement Strategy: Use GPT to develop a client engagement strategy for upselling and cross-selling. *Prompt:* "Create a strategy to upsell and cross-sell additional AI consulting services to existing clients." *Response:* GPT suggests personalized service bundles based on client project histories, industry trends, and identified business needs to maximize service expansion opportunities.

Cost Control

Continuously monitor and control your costs to maintain profitability. GPT can analyze expense data and identify cost-saving measures.

Example:

o Cost Optimization Plan: Use GPT to create a cost optimization plan. *Prompt:* "Develop a plan to optimize costs and improve profitability in our AI consulting practice." *Response:* GPT provides cost-saving recommendations such as resource utilization tracking, supplier negotiation strategies, and operational efficiency improvements to achieve financial goals.

Actionable Insight:

o Implement a cloud-based accounting system to track expenses, manage invoices, and generate financial reports, providing greater visibility into your financial health. *Prompt:* "Transition to a cloud-based accounting system to streamline financial management processes." *Response:* GPT outlines steps including software selection, data migration procedures, and staff training to enhance financial transparency and efficiency.

By utilizing GPT to manage business risks, ensure data privacy and security, and maximize profitability, generative AI consultants can navigate challenges effectively while optimizing operational efficiency and client satisfaction.

Chapter 12

The Future of Generative AI Consulting

The future of generative AI consulting hinges on embracing emerging trends and continuous learning to maintain relevance and competitiveness in a rapidly evolving industry. Leveraging GPT can facilitate staying ahead of these trends and fostering a culture of innovation within your consulting practice.

Emerging Trends in AI and GPT

Staying abreast of emerging trends in AI is pivotal for shaping the future direction of your consulting practice. Key trends include:

Investment

As of May 2023, according to the latest update from NEX's *Generative Open-source Market Map*, over $66 billion dollars across 600 investments listed had been invested in generative Ai companies and start-ups. This trend supports huge growth potential for consultants, as new start-ups in multiple industries will be looking for consultative services to help them succeed in this new generative AI-driven landscape. We view this as a very unique opportunity in this emerging market.

AI Ethics and Governance

There is a growing emphasis on ethical AI practices and the development of governance frameworks to ensure responsible AI deployment. GPT can assist in developing ethical guidelines and governance frameworks tailored to specific client needs and regulatory requirements.

Example:

o Ethical AI Framework: Use GPT to develop an ethical AI framework for client projects. *Prompt*: "Create an ethical AI framework that aligns with regulatory standards and promotes responsible AI use." *Response*: GPT generates a framework outlining principles such as fairness, transparency, and accountability in AI decision-making processes, tailored to industry-specific ethical considerations.

Explainable AI (XAI)

Advancements in explainable AI (XAI) are crucial for improving transparency and fostering trust in AI systems. GPT can explain complex AI models and decisions in understandable terms, enhancing client understanding and acceptance.

Example:

o XAI Implementation Strategy: Use GPT to outline an XAI implementation strategy. *Prompt*: "Develop a strategy to implement explainable AI techniques in our consulting projects to improve transparency." *Response*: GPT suggests methods such as model interpretability techniques, interactive visualizations, and client workshops to enhance transparency and user trust in AI solutions.

AI and Automation

The integration of AI with automation technologies is accelerating, offering opportunities to streamline processes and boost operational efficiency. GPT can recommend AI-driven automation solutions tailored to optimize client workflows and business operations.

Example:

o AI-Driven Automation Proposal: Use GPT to propose AI-driven automation solutions. *Prompt*: "Recommend AI-powered automation solutions to enhance operational efficiency in client organizations." *Response*: GPT identifies automation opportunities such as robotic process automation (RPA), AI-powered predictive analytics, and intelligent document processing to streamline client workflows and drive business efficiency.

Actionable Insight:

76

- o Regularly research and stay updated on emerging trends in AI through industry publications, conferences, and online resources to ensure your consulting practice remains at the forefront of innovation. *Prompt*: "Develop a plan for staying updated on emerging AI trends and technologies." *Response*: GPT suggests subscribing to AI industry newsletters, attending AI conferences, and participating in webinars on emerging AI topics to maintain knowledge currency and industry leadership.

Continuous Learning and Development

Continuous learning and development are paramount for staying competitive in the dynamic field of AI consulting. Strategies include:

Lifelong Learning

Commit to lifelong learning by continuously updating skills and knowledge through courses, certifications, and professional development programs. GPT can recommend relevant learning opportunities based on individual career goals and industry trends.

Example:

- o Professional Development Roadmap: Use GPT to create a professional development roadmap. *Prompt*: "Develop a roadmap for continuous professional development in AI consulting." *Response*: GPT outlines a roadmap including AI certification programs, advanced machine learning courses, and specialized workshops to enhance skills in emerging AI areas.

Knowledge Sharing

Foster a culture of knowledge sharing within your team and with clients to promote continuous learning and collaboration. GPT can facilitate the creation of knowledge sharing platforms and resources.

Example:

- o Knowledge Sharing Platform: Use GPT to design a knowledge sharing platform. *Prompt*: "Create a platform for sharing AI insights and best practices with our team and clients." *Response*: GPT suggests developing a centralized knowledge repository with curated

AI articles, case studies, and interactive forums to facilitate continuous learning and expertise exchange.

Adaptability

Stay adaptable and open to new ideas and approaches to effectively respond to industry changes and client demands. GPT can analyze market trends and recommend adaptive strategies to pivot business approaches as needed.

Example:

- o Adaptation Strategy: Use GPT to develop an adaptive business strategy. *Prompt*: "Develop a strategy to adapt to evolving AI trends and client needs." *Response*: GPT proposes strategies such as agile project management frameworks, rapid prototyping methodologies, and flexible service offerings to maintain responsiveness and competitiveness.

Actionable Insight:

- o Set aside dedicated time each month for professional development activities such as attending webinars, reading industry publications, and participating in online courses to ensure continuous learning and adaptation to industry changes. *Prompt*: "Create a schedule for ongoing professional development activities." *Response*: GPT generates a calendar with monthly activities including AI webinars, industry conferences, and specialized training sessions to foster continuous learning and professional growth.

By leveraging GPT to navigate emerging AI trends, foster continuous learning, and adapt to industry changes, generative AI consultants can position themselves as leaders in innovation while delivering value-driven solutions to clients.

Chapter 13

Conclusion

Recap of Key Points

In this comprehensive guide, we have embarked on a journey toward becoming a successful generative AI consultant. Let's recap the key points covered throughout the chapters:

1. Fundamentals of Generative AI and Applications
    o   Explored the foundational concepts of generative AI and its diverse applications across industries.
    o   Discussed how generative AI can create value through content generation, data synthesis, and personalized recommendations.
2. Building Technical and Business Skills
    o   Emphasized the importance of acquiring both technical skills (e.g., machine learning, natural language processing) and business skills (e.g., project management, client communication).
    o   Highlighted the role of continuous learning in staying abreast of technological advancements and industry best practices.
3. Client Acquisition and Relationship Management
    o   Strategized on identifying client needs, demonstrating expertise, and building trust through effective communication and solution-oriented approaches.
    o   Explored techniques for nurturing client relationships and maintaining client satisfaction throughout project lifecycles.
4. Developing a Robust Business Plan

o Outlined the components of a robust business plan, including defining services, target markets, competitive analysis, and financial projections.

o Discussed strategies for managing finances, budgeting, and monitoring financial performance to ensure sustainability and growth.

5. Effective Marketing Strategies

o Explored various marketing channels and tactics tailored to promoting generative AI consulting services.

o Highlighted the importance of crafting a compelling value proposition and leveraging digital platforms, content marketing, and networking to enhance visibility and attract clients.

6. Efficient Project Management and Collaboration

o Detailed project management techniques such as agile methodologies, task management tools, and client collaboration strategies.

o Emphasized the significance of clear communication, regular updates, and iterative feedback loops to ensure successful project outcomes.

7. Scaling Your Business

o Strategies for scaling a generative AI consulting practice through service expansion, geographic reach, and strategic partnerships.

o Insights into building a talented team, fostering a positive organizational culture, and maintaining service quality amid growth.

8. Risk Management, Data Privacy, and Profitability
o Addressed risk identification, mitigation strategies, and the importance of insurance coverage in safeguarding business operations.

o Discussed implementing robust data privacy measures, compliance with regulations, and strategies for maximizing profitability through value-based pricing and cost control.

9. Staying Ahead of Emerging Trends

o Explored emerging trends in AI, including AI ethics, explainable AI, and AI automation, and their implications for generative AI consulting.

o Advocated for continuous learning, adaptability, and proactive market monitoring to capitalize on industry shifts and technological advancements.

Final Thoughts

Becoming a successful generative AI consultant demands a multifaceted approach blending technical prowess with business acumen and a commitment to continuous improvement. By embracing the strategies and best practices outlined in this book, you are empowered to build a thriving consulting practice that not only meets but exceeds client expectations while advancing the frontiers of AI innovation.

Insights and Findings:

- Integration of Skills: The intersection of technical expertise in AI with effective business management skills forms the foundation for sustainable consulting success.

- Client-Centric Approach: Understanding and addressing client needs through tailored solutions and proactive communication are pivotal to forging long-term client partnerships.

- Strategic Growth: Scaling a consulting practice requires strategic foresight, including expanding service offerings, entering new markets, and forming strategic alliances.

- Risk Management and Compliance: Prioritizing risk management, data privacy, and regulatory compliance safeguards your business reputation and enhances client trust.

- Adaptability and Innovation: Staying ahead in the rapidly evolving AI landscape necessitates continuous learning, embracing emerging technologies, and adapting business strategies to seize new opportunities.

In conclusion, as you embark on your journey as a generative AI consultant, remember that success is not just about technical proficiency but also about fostering innovation, building lasting client relationships, and contributing positively to the transformative impact of AI technologies across industries. By applying the knowledge gained from this guide and remaining agile in your approach, you are poised to navigate challenges, capitalize on opportunities, and achieve sustained growth in the dynamic field of generative AI consulting.

Appendix 1

Example Consulting Scenario

Example Scenario:

Becoming a generative AI consultant is an exciting endeavor, especially with the focus on integrating generative AI into consulting practices. Given the knowledge you have gained from the book, let's create an example scenario for a consultant analyzing **XYZ Consulting Corporation**, with the goal of integrating generative AI into their practice. They want to enhance operational efficiency, innovation, and client service delivery. This example will follow the 7-step consulting process adapted for the generative AI integration context and will utilize ChatGPT to help produce analytics and deliverables.

Step 1: Define the Objective

- **Objective**: To integrate generative AI technologies into XYZ Consulting Corporation's services to enhance efficiency, innovation, and client engagement.
- **Consultant Task:** Analyze the company's current service offerings and technology stack to identify opportunities for generative AI integration.

Step 2: Gather Data

- **Consultant Task**: Conduct interviews with key stakeholders and review existing technology infrastructure. Collect data on current challenges, technology gaps, and areas where AI could enhance decision-making, creativity, or operational processes.

Step 3: Analyze the Situation

- **Consultant Task**: Evaluate the collected data to understand where generative AI can provide the most value. This could involve enhancing data analysis capabilities, automating routine tasks, or generating innovative solutions for client problems.

Step 4: Gap Analysis

- **Description**: Identify gaps between the current use of technology at XYZ Consulting and the potential applications of generative AI.
- **Consultant Task**: Compare current practices against industry benchmarks for AI integration and identify areas for improvement.
- **Output**: A gap analysis report highlighting areas where generative AI can be integrated to improve services and operations.

Step 5: Develop Recommendations

- **Consultant Task**: Based on the gap analysis, develop actionable recommendations for integrating generative AI tools. This might include specific AI technologies for data analysis, content generation, or process automation.
- **Example Recommendation**: Implement a generative AI tool for automating market research reports, reducing time spent on manual data compilation and analysis.

Step 6: Develop Corresponding Implementation Plan

- **Consultant Task**: Create a detailed plan outlining the steps for integrating recommended generative AI technologies. This plan should include timelines, required resources, responsible parties, and success metrics.
- **Example Implementation Step**: Pilot the generative AI market research tool with a small team, evaluate its impact on report generation efficiency, and plan a full rollout based on feedback.

Step 7: Feedback & Review

- **Consultant Task**: Establish a feedback mechanism to monitor the effectiveness of the generative AI integration. Gather feedback from both the consulting team and clients on the AI tools' impact.

84

- **Example Feedback Plan**: Conduct monthly review sessions to discuss the generative AI tools' performance, gather suggestions for improvement, and adjust the implementation plan as necessary.

Generative AI Integration Proposal for XYZ Consulting

- **Task**: Using the 7-step process and leveraging ChatGPT, develop a proposal for integrating generative AI at XYZ Consulting. Your proposal should include a detailed gap analysis, actionable recommendations, and a step-by-step implementation plan.
- **Deliverables**:

  o   Gap Analysis Report

  o   Generative AI Integration Recommendations

  o   Implementation Plan

  o   Feedback and Review Mechanism Proposal

Quality Assessment Criteria

- **Understanding of Generative AI Applications**: Solution demonstrates a clear understanding of how generative AI can be applied in a consulting context.
- **Analytical Rigor**: Shows thorough analysis in the gap analysis and recommendations phases.
- **Practicality and Creativity**: Proposes realistic, innovative solutions that can be practically implemented.
- **Clarity and Structure**: Presents a well-structured and clear proposal with actionable steps.

This example scenario for becoming a successful generative AI consultant provides a comprehensive framework for candidates to apply their knowledge in a real-world context, preparing them to tackle similar challenges in their consulting careers.

Appendix 2

GEN AI Consulting Fields

Business Consulting Services

There are two broad categories of consulting services, each with overlap: **business consulting** and **consumer consulting**. Let's look at the larger group first: business consulting.

In addition to a specialty, a business consulting service may decide to specialize in one of two approaches to advising clients. The service may *emphasize the resolution of an issue* or *the transfer of needed skills to the client*. For example, a restaurant with cash flow problems may only need advice on how to resolve that specific problem. Or the owner may need to be trained in advanced cash flow forecasting and other aspects of business management.

There are advantages and disadvantages to both approaches for the consultant and the client. Problem resolution is less expensive for the client, but it may not solve the underlying cause. Skill transfer is more expensive for the client, but it reduces dependence on the consultant.

Personal Consulting

Businesses aren't the only clients for useful advice. Consumers also need informed help making decisions. The following is a list of common personal consulting services. Personal consulting services could include:

- Adventure travel

- Aerobics

- Beauty

- Career

- Childcare

- College entrance

- Credit
- Cruises
- Dog training
- Estate planning
- Event planning
- Family relations
- Family travel
- Fashion
- Fitness
- Gardening
- Golf
- Health services
- Home buying
- Home remodeling
- Home repair
- Honeymoons
- Image
- Interior decorating
- Interior design
- Journal writing
- Landscaping
- Makeover
- Marriage relations
- Medical

- Music

- Party planning

- Personal image

- Personal trainer

- Pet selection

- Photography

- Poker

- Religion

- Relocation

- Resume

- Spiritual

- Studying

- Taxes

- Voice

- Wardrobe

- Wedding

- Weight loss

- Women's issues

- Woodworking

These are just a few of the hundreds of topics on which consumers want help.

Within these fields, there are many areas of specialization that can be selected to fit your client's needs as well as your own interests and skills. What do you know that others would pay to know?

Consumer consultants aren't typically paid as much as business consultants. The primary reason is that a business can financially benefit from useful advice, so it is in a position to pay more for that advice. In addition, credentials for a business consultant are often more difficult and expensive to acquire that those for a consumer consultant. Even so, a consumer consultant with strong credentials and valuable advice serving a specific market can make an excellent income.

Ai-Enhanced Applications: By incorporating generative AI into these subjects, consultants can provide valuable insights, solutions, and tools that can transform and optimize various aspects of a business.

1. Strategy Consulting:

    o Applying generative AI for strategic decision-making, such as generating alternative scenarios and evaluating their potential outcomes.

    o Utilizing generative AI models to simulate and optimize business strategies based on different variables and constraints.

2. Operations Consulting:

    o Implementing generative AI algorithms for demand forecasting, production planning, and inventory optimization to improve operational efficiency.
    o Developing generative AI models to automate and optimize supply chain management, including demand-supply matching and logistics optimization.

3. Financial Consulting:

    o Using generative AI to forecast financial trends and market dynamics, enabling better investment strategies and risk management.

    o Applying generative AI for fraud detection and anomaly detection in financial transactions, improving security and minimizing financial losses.

4. Human Resources Consulting:

- o Utilizing generative AI models for talent acquisition, automating candidate screening and resume analysis to streamline the recruitment process.

- o Implementing generative AI algorithms for employee performance analysis and personalized learning programs, enhancing workforce productivity and engagement.

5. Marketing and Sales Consulting:

- o Leveraging generative AI for customer segmentation and targeted marketing, enabling personalized campaigns and better customer engagement.

- o Developing generative AI models for content generation, including automated writing, image synthesis, and video creation, to enhance marketing efforts.

6. Technology Consulting:

- o Assisting businesses in the adoption and integration of generative AI technologies, including model selection, implementation, and optimization.

- o Providing expertise in applying generative AI for natural language processing, computer vision, and other specialized areas to enhance product development and customer experience.

7. Change Management Consulting:

- o Helping organizations navigate the impact of generative AI on their operations and workforce, including addressing concerns, training employees, and managing change resistance.

- o Developing strategies to leverage generative AI for innovation and competitive advantage while maintaining a smooth transition and organizational culture.

o   Supporting businesses in understanding and addressing the ethical and social implications of generative AI implementation, ensuring responsible and sustainable use.

8. Sustainability Consulting:

o   Utilizing generative AI to optimize energy consumption, resource allocation, and waste management, contributing to sustainable business practices.

o   Applying generative AI models for environmental impact assessment and mitigation strategies, aiding organizations in their sustainability efforts.

9. Risk Management Consulting:

o   Utilizing generative AI models to simulate and predict potential risks and their impact on business operations, enabling proactive risk management strategies.

o   Developing generative AI algorithms for fraud detection, anomaly detection, and risk assessment, improving the effectiveness of risk mitigation measures.

10. Supply Chain Consulting:

o   Applying generative AI for demand forecasting and inventory optimization, enabling businesses to optimize their supply chain operations and reduce costs.

o   Developing generative AI models to optimize route planning, transportation scheduling, and warehouse management, improving overall supply chain efficiency.

11. Innovation Consulting:

o   Leveraging generative AI for idea generation and concept development, enabling businesses to explore and create new products, services, and business models.

o   Applying generative AI algorithms for predictive analytics and trend analysis to identify emerging opportunities and market trends, fostering innovation.

12. Process Improvement Consulting:

   o Utilizing generative AI to identify bottlenecks and inefficiencies in business processes, enabling data-driven process optimization and automation.

   o Developing generative AI models for predictive maintenance and quality control, minimizing downtime and improving product quality.

13. Auto Sales Training/Consulting:

   o Utilizing generative AI for personalized vehicle recommendations and pricing optimization, enhancing customer experiences and improving sales conversions.

   o Applying generative AI models for automated customer segmentation and targeted marketing campaigns, aiding in reaching the right audience with the right vehicle offers.

14. Business Selling:

   o Applying generative AI for customer segmentation and lead scoring, enabling businesses to identify high-potential prospects and optimize sales efforts.

   o Utilizing generative AI models for automated sales proposal generation and customization, improving the effectiveness of sales presentations.

15. Business Start-up Consulting:

   o Developing generative AI models for business idea generation and evaluation, assisting entrepreneurs in identifying viable startup opportunities.

   o Applying generative AI for market research and analysis, aiding startups in understanding customer needs, market trends, and competitive landscapes.

16. Business Travel:

- o Utilizing generative AI for travel itinerary optimization and personalized recommendations, improving the efficiency and experience of business travel.

- o Developing generative AI algorithms for real-time travel risk assessment and mitigation, enhancing traveler safety and security.

17. Business Writing:

- o Applying generative AI for automated content generation, assisting businesses in producing high-quality written content for various purposes, such as blog posts, articles, and reports.

- o Utilizing generative AI models for language adaptation and editing, aiding writers in refining their business writing style and ensuring clarity and coherence.

18. Business Selling:

- o Applying generative AI for customer segmentation and lead scoring, enabling businesses to identify high-potential prospects and optimize sales efforts.

- o Utilizing generative AI models for automated sales proposal generation and customization, improving the effectiveness of sales presentations.

19. Customer Experience Consulting:

- o Applying generative AI for sentiment analysis and customer feedback analysis, enabling businesses to gain insights into customer preferences and improve their experience.

- o Developing generative AI models for chatbots and virtual assistants to provide personalized and interactive customer support, enhancing customer satisfaction.

20. Cybersecurity Consulting:

- o Utilizing generative AI models for anomaly detection and intrusion detection, enhancing the ability to identify and respond to cybersecurity threats.

- o Developing generative AI algorithms for automated threat hunting and security incident response, improving the efficiency and effectiveness of cybersecurity measures.

21. Compliance Consulting:

- o Applying generative AI for regulatory compliance monitoring and reporting, automating compliance processes and reducing manual effort.

- o Developing generative AI models for risk-based compliance assessment and prediction, helping businesses proactively identify and address compliance risks.

22. Data Analytics Consulting:

- o Leveraging generative AI algorithms for data synthesis and augmentation, enhancing the quality and quantity of available data for analysis.

- o Applying generative AI for exploratory data analysis and pattern recognition, uncovering hidden insights and improving decision-making.

23. Data Processing Consulting:

- o Utilizing generative AI for automated data cleansing and preprocessing, improving data quality and accuracy for analysis and decision-making.

- o Developing generative AI models for automated data categorization and feature extraction, aiding businesses in extracting valuable insights from large datasets.

24. Direct Marketing Consulting:

- o Applying generative AI for customer profiling and segmentation in direct marketing campaigns, enabling targeted and personalized marketing communications.

- o Utilizing generative AI models for automated campaign content generation and optimization, improving the effectiveness of direct marketing initiatives.

25. E-Business Consulting:

- o Developing generative AI models for personalized product recommendations and dynamic pricing in e-commerce, enhancing customer engagement and conversion rates.

- o Applying generative AI for automated chatbot and virtual assistant services, improving customer support and online shopping experiences.

26. Economic Research Consulting:

- o Utilizing generative AI for predictive modeling and scenario analysis in economic forecasting, aiding researchers in making accurate economic predictions.

- o Developing generative AI models for automated data analysis and interpretation, enabling researchers to extract insights and trends from economic data more efficiently.

27. Editorial Process Consulting:

- o Applying generative AI for automated content editing and proofreading, improving the quality and consistency of written materials in editorial processes.

- o Utilizing generative AI models for style adaptation and language refinement, assisting editors in maintaining the desired tone and voice across various editorial projects.

28. Education:

- o Applying generative AI for automated content generation and lesson planning, aiding in the creation of engaging and personalized educational materials.

- o Utilizing generative AI models for intelligent tutoring systems and adaptive learning platforms, enhancing student learning experiences and outcomes.

29. Employee Benefit Consulting:

   o Developing generative AI models for personalized employee benefits recommendations based on individual needs and preferences.

   o Applying generative AI for automated benefits enrollment and administration, streamlining the process and reducing administrative overhead.

30. Engineering Consulting:

   o Utilizing generative AI for automated design optimization and product innovation in engineering projects, accelerating the design process and improving efficiency.

   o Developing generative AI models for predictive maintenance and fault detection in engineering systems, enhancing reliability and reducing downtime.

31. Environmental Consulting:

   o Applying generative AI for environmental data analysis and prediction, aiding in the assessment and management of environmental risks and impacts.

   o Utilizing generative AI models for automated environmental impact assessments and sustainability reporting, assisting businesses in meeting regulatory requirements.

32. Executive Search Consulting:

   o Utilizing generative AI for talent profiling and executive candidate matching, aiding executive search firms in identifying suitable candidates for senior-level positions.

   o Applying generative AI models for automated assessment of leadership traits and competencies, improving the effectiveness of executive search processes.

33. Financial Management Consulting:

- o Developing generative AI models for automated financial analysis and forecasting, assisting businesses in making data-driven financial decisions and improving financial performance.

- o Applying generative AI for risk assessment and portfolio optimization in financial management, aiding in investment decision-making and risk mitigation.

34. Food Services Consulting:

    - o Utilizing generative AI for menu optimization and personalized recommendations, improving customer satisfaction and driving revenue in the food services industry.

    - o Applying generative AI models for automated food quality monitoring and safety compliance, ensuring high-quality and safe food offerings.

35. Foreclosure Consulting:

    - o Developing generative AI models for automated foreclosure risk assessment and prediction, aiding in proactive foreclosure prevention measures and intervention strategies.

    - o Applying generative AI for automated documentation generation and compliance tracking in foreclosure processes, streamlining foreclosure proceedings.

36. Forestry Consulting:

    - o Utilizing generative AI for forest resource mapping and monitoring, aiding in sustainable forest management and timber yield optimization.

    - o Developing generative AI models for automated tree species identification and disease detection, assisting in early intervention and forest conservation efforts.

37. Franchising Consulting:

- o Applying generative AI for location analysis and market potential assessment in franchising decisions, aiding in identifying suitable franchise locations.

- o Utilizing generative AI models for automated franchisee selection and compatibility assessment, ensuring successful franchise partnerships.

38. Fundraising Consulting:

- o Developing generative AI models for donor segmentation and personalized fundraising strategies, enabling organizations to optimize fundraising efforts and donor engagement.

- o Applying generative AI for automated donor behavior analysis and predictive modeling, aiding in identifying potential major donors and optimizing fundraising campaigns.

39. Gaming Consulting:

- o Utilizing generative AI for game design and content generation, automating the creation of game levels, characters, and narratives.

- o Developing generative AI models for player behavior analysis and personalized gaming experiences, enhancing player engagement and satisfaction.

40. Government Relations Consulting:

- o Applying generative AI for sentiment analysis and social media monitoring in government relations, aiding in understanding public sentiment and managing public perception.

- o Utilizing generative AI models for automated policy analysis

41. Grant Writing Consulting:

- Applying generative AI for automated grant proposal generation and customization, improving the quality and effectiveness of grant applications.

- Utilizing generative AI models for grant opportunity identification and matching, assisting organizations in finding relevant funding opportunities.

42. Graphic Design Consulting:

- Developing generative AI algorithms and utilizing plug-ins for automated graphic design and layout generation, enabling businesses to create visually appealing designs efficiently.

- Applying generative AI for image synthesis and style transfer, assisting graphic designers in creating unique and customized visual content.

43. Hospital Administration Consulting:

- Utilizing generative AI for patient flow optimization and resource allocation in hospital operations, improving efficiency and patient satisfaction.

- Applying generative AI models for predictive analytics in healthcare demand forecasting and capacity planning, aiding in proactive management of patient needs.

44. Hotel Management Consulting:

- Developing generative AI models for personalized guest recommendations and dynamic pricing in hotel management, enhancing guest experiences and revenue generation.

- Applying generative AI for automated hotel room allocation and reservation management, optimizing occupancy rates and room assignment efficiency.

45. Human Resources Consulting:

o Applying generative AI for candidate screening and automated resume analysis, improving the efficiency and accuracy of recruitment processes.

o Utilizing generative AI models for employee sentiment analysis and engagement prediction, aiding in proactive HR interventions and talent retention.

46. Immigration Consulting:

o Developing generative AI models for automated visa application assistance and immigration document processing, streamlining immigration procedures and reducing errors.

o Applying generative AI for sentiment analysis and public opinion monitoring in immigration policy discussions, aiding in understanding public sentiment and informing policy decisions.

47. Information Technology Consulting:

o Utilizing generative AI for automated code generation and software development, accelerating the software development process and reducing coding effort.

o Applying generative AI models for anomaly detection and cybersecurity threat analysis, enhancing IT security and incident response capabilities.

48. Insurance:

o Developing generative AI models for automated insurance claim processing and fraud detection, improving efficiency and accuracy in the insurance industry.

o Applying generative AI for personalized insurance product recommendations and risk assessment, enhancing customer experience and underwriting accuracy.

49. Inventory Control:

- o Utilizing generative AI for demand forecasting and inventory optimization, aiding in effective inventory management and reducing stockouts and excess inventory.

- o Developing generative AI models for automated inventory classification and replenishment decision-making, improving supply chain efficiency.

50. Investments:

- o Applying generative AI for automated investment portfolio analysis and optimization, aiding in making data-driven investment decisions and maximizing returns.

- o Utilizing generative AI models for automated trading and investment strategy generation, enhancing investment performance and risk management.

51. Labor Relations:

- o Developing generative AI models for sentiment analysis and employee feedback monitoring in labor relations, aiding in understanding employee sentiment and improving employee relations.

- o Applying generative AI for predictive modeling of labor disputes and conflict resolution strategies, assisting in proactive labor relations management.

52. Land-Use Planning:

- o Utilizing generative AI for land-use classification and zoning optimization, aiding in efficient land-use planning and development.

- o Applying generative AI models for predictive modeling of environmental impacts and urban development patterns, informing land-use planning decisions.

53. Leasing:

o Developing generative AI models for automated lease agreement generation and contract analysis, improving efficiency and accuracy in leasing processes.

o Applying generative AI for automated lease recommendation and negotiation strategies, aiding in optimizing lease agreements for both parties involved.

54. Legal Services:

o Developing generative AI models for legal document analysis and contract review, aiding in due diligence processes and improving accuracy and efficiency.

o Applying generative AI for legal research and case analysis, assisting lawyers in identifying relevant legal precedents and optimizing legal strategies.

55. Licensing:

o Utilizing generative AI for automated license agreement analysis and compliance tracking, ensuring adherence to licensing regulations and obligations.

o Developing generative AI models for license recommendation and optimization based on user preferences and requirements, assisting in license selection and acquisition.

56. Mail Order:

o Applying generative AI for automated order fulfillment and shipping optimization in mail-order businesses, improving operational efficiency and customer satisfaction.

o Utilizing generative AI models for customer segmentation and personalized marketing strategies in mail-order marketing campaigns, enhancing customer engagement and conversion rates.

57. Management:

- o Developing generative AI models for decision support and management strategy analysis, aiding in making data-driven management decisions and optimizing business performance.

- o Applying generative AI for sentiment analysis and employee feedback monitoring, assisting in understanding organizational dynamics and improving managerial effectiveness.

58. Marketing:

- o Utilizing generative AI for personalized marketing content generation and dynamic campaign optimization, improving customer engagement and marketing effectiveness.

- o Developing generative AI models for market trend analysis and predictive modeling, aiding in identifying market opportunities and optimizing marketing strategies.

59. Material Handling:

- o Applying generative AI for automated warehouse layout optimization and inventory routing, improving efficiency in material handling and reducing operational costs.

- o Utilizing generative AI models for predictive analytics in supply chain management, aiding in demand forecasting and resource allocation for material handling operations.

60. Mergers and Acquisitions:

- o Developing generative AI models for merger and acquisition target identification and valuation, aiding in making informed investment decisions and assessing potential synergies.

- o Applying generative AI for automated due diligence and risk assessment in mergers and acquisitions, improving efficiency and accuracy in the evaluation process.

61. Office Management:

- o Utilizing generative AI for automated office space planning and layout optimization, enhancing workspace efficiency and employee productivity.

- o Developing generative AI models for automated task assignment and scheduling in office management, improving workflow and resource allocation.

62. Online Business:

- o Applying generative AI for automated product recommendations and personalized customer experiences in online businesses, enhancing customer satisfaction and retention.

- o Utilizing generative AI models for automated chatbots and virtual assistants in online customer support, improving customer service and response times.

63. Operations:

- o Developing generative AI models for automated operations process optimization and resource allocation, improving efficiency and reducing operational costs.

- o Applying generative AI for predictive analytics and anomaly detection in operations management, aiding in proactive maintenance and quality control.

64. Opinion Polling:

- o Utilizing generative AI for sentiment analysis and opinion mining in opinion polls, aiding in understanding public sentiment and opinion dynamics.

- o Developing generative AI models for automated survey generation and analysis, improving the accuracy and efficiency of opinion polling processes.

65. Organizational Development:

- o Applying generative AI for talent development and succession planning, aiding in identifying high-potential employees and facilitating their professional growth.

- o Utilizing generative AI models for sentiment analysis and organizational culture assessment, assisting in understanding organizational dynamics and facilitating change.

66. Payroll Management:

- o Developing generative AI models for automated payroll calculation and tax compliance, improving accuracy and efficiency in payroll management.

- o Applying generative AI for employee time tracking and attendance monitoring, streamlining payroll processes and reducing manual effort.

67. Performance:

- o Utilizing generative AI for automated performance data analysis and employee performance evaluation, aiding in identifying strengths, weaknesses, and improvement areas.

- o Developing generative AI models for personalized performance improvement recommendations and training programs, enhancing employee development and productivity.

68. Political:

- o Applying generative AI for sentiment analysis and public opinion monitoring in political campaigns, aiding in understanding public sentiment and informing campaign strategies.

- o Utilizing generative AI models for personalized political messaging and voter targeting, enhancing campaign effectiveness and voter engagement.

69. Pollution Control:

- o Developing generative AI models for environmental impact assessment and pollution mitigation strategies, aiding in proactive pollution control measures and compliance.

- o Applying generative AI for predictive modeling of pollution patterns and pollutant source identification, assisting in targeted pollution control efforts.

70. Product Design:

- o Utilizing generative AI for automated design optimization and innovation, assisting in creating efficient, user-friendly, and aesthetically appealing product designs.

- o Applying generative AI models for virtual prototyping and simulation, aiding in rapid iteration and testing of product designs.

71. Project Management:

- o Developing generative AI models for project risk assessment and mitigation strategies, aiding in proactive management of potential project risks and issues.

- o Applying generative AI for automated project scheduling and resource allocation, optimizing project timelines and improving resource utilization.

72. Quality Control:

- o Applying generative AI for automated quality inspection and defect detection in manufacturing processes, improving product quality and reducing waste.

- o Utilizing generative AI models for predictive analytics in quality control, aiding in proactive maintenance and process optimization to ensure consistent quality.

73. Real Estate Investment:

- o Developing generative AI models for real estate market analysis and property valuation, aiding in making informed investment decisions and assessing potential returns.

- o Applying generative AI for automated property search and recommendation systems, assisting investors in identifying suitable real estate investment opportunities.

74. Recycling:

- o Utilizing generative AI for automated waste sorting and recycling optimization, improving recycling processes and reducing environmental impact.

- o Developing generative AI models for automated recycling facility optimization and resource allocation, aiding in efficient recycling operations.

75. Rehabilitation:

- o Applying generative AI for personalized rehabilitation program design and progress tracking, enhancing patient outcomes and rehabilitation efficiency.

- o Utilizing generative AI models for automated analysis of patient rehabilitation data and treatment recommendations, aiding in optimizing rehabilitation protocols.

76. Restaurant Management:

- o Developing generative AI models for menu optimization, pricing strategies, and ingredient substitution recommendations in restaurant management, improving profitability and customer satisfaction.

- o Applying generative AI for demand forecasting and table optimization, aiding in efficient restaurant capacity planning and reservation management.

77. Retailing:

- o Utilizing generative AI for personalized product recommendations and dynamic pricing strategies in retail, enhancing customer engagement and driving sales.

- o Developing generative AI models for automated inventory management and supply chain optimization, improving retail operations and reducing stockouts.

78. Reunion Planning:

- o Applying generative AI for automated venue selection and reunion activity recommendations, aiding in planning and organizing successful reunions.

- o Utilizing generative AI models for attendee sentiment analysis and personalized event experiences, enhancing the reunion experience for attendees.

79. Safety:

- o Applying generative AI for real-time monitoring and analysis of safety data, enabling proactive identification of potential hazards and risks.

- o Developing generative AI models for predictive maintenance of safety equipment and systems, ensuring optimal safety measures are in place.

80. Salary Administration:

- o Utilizing generative AI for salary benchmarking and compensation analysis, enabling organizations to make data-driven decisions in salary administration.

- o Developing generative AI algorithms for automated salary structure design and optimization, ensuring fair and competitive compensation practices.

81. Sales:

- o Applying generative AI for sales forecasting and demand prediction, enabling businesses to optimize sales strategies and resource allocation.

o Utilizing generative AI models for personalized sales recommendations and cross-selling opportunities, enhancing customer engagement and conversion rates.

82. Sanitation:

o Developing generative AI models for waste detection and management in sanitation systems, improving operational efficiency and waste reduction efforts.

o Utilizing generative AI for predictive maintenance of sanitation equipment and infrastructure, minimizing downtime and optimizing resource allocation.

83. Security:

o Applying generative AI for video surveillance and anomaly detection, enhancing security monitoring capabilities and threat identification.

o Utilizing generative AI models for biometric identification and access control, improving security measures and preventing unauthorized access.

84. Search Engine Optimization (SEO):

o Developing generative AI algorithms for keyword research and content optimization, improving website ranking and visibility in search engine results.

o Applying generative AI for automated SEO audits and recommendations, assisting businesses in optimizing their online presence and driving organic traffic.

85. Shipping:

o Utilizing generative AI for route optimization and delivery scheduling, minimizing transportation costs and improving delivery efficiency.

o Developing generative AI models for predictive analytics in shipping logistics, enabling proactive management of delays, disruptions, and capacity planning.

86. Small Business:

   o Applying generative AI for customer segmentation and targeted marketing strategies tailored to the unique needs of small businesses.

   o Utilizing generative AI models for automated financial analysis and forecasting, assisting small businesses in making data-driven decisions and managing cash flow.

87. Social Services:

   o Developing generative AI models for needs assessment and resource allocation in social service programs, optimizing service delivery and impact.

   o Applying generative AI for sentiment analysis and social media monitoring, aiding social service organizations in understanding public sentiment and improving engagement.

88. Stockholder Relations:

   o Utilizing generative AI for sentiment analysis and predictive modeling in stockholder communications, improving investor relations and decision-making.

   o Applying generative AI algorithms for automated reporting and analysis of financial data, enhancing transparency and communication with stockholders.

89. Strategic Planning:

   o Developing generative AI models for scenario analysis and strategic decision support, aiding organizations in evaluating potential outcomes and formulating effective strategies.

   o Applying generative AI for market trend analysis and competitive intelligence, enabling businesses to identify emerging opportunities and threats.

90. Tax Law:

110

- o Utilizing generative AI for tax compliance monitoring and analysis, automating tax-related processes and reducing the risk of errors.

- o Applying generative AI models for tax planning and optimization, assisting businesses in identifying tax-saving opportunities and managing tax liabilities.

91. Technical Writing:

- o Developing generative AI models for automated content generation and technical documentation, improving the efficiency and quality of technical writing processes.

- o Utilizing generative AI for language translation and localization of technical documents, enabling businesses to reach a global audience effectively.

92. Telecommunications:

- o Applying generative AI for network optimization and predictive maintenance, improving the reliability and performance of telecommunications infrastructure.

- o Utilizing generative AI models for customer churn prediction and targeted marketing campaigns, enhancing customer retention and revenue generation.

93. Traffic Control:

- o Developing generative AI algorithms for traffic flow prediction and congestion management, optimizing traffic control strategies and reducing travel times.

- o Applying generative AI for real-time incident detection and response in traffic management systems, improving overall traffic safety and efficiency.

94. Training Consulting:

- o Utilizing generative AI for personalized training program design and content generation, tailoring training materials to individual learner needs.

o Developing generative AI models for automated assessment and feedback in training programs, providing real-time performance evaluation and adaptive learning experiences.

95. Translation:

o Utilizing generative AI for automated translation services, enabling businesses to translate content quickly and accurately across multiple languages.

o Developing generative AI models for natural language processing and language generation, improving the quality and fluency of translated text.

96. Urban Renewal:

o Applying generative AI for urban planning and design, facilitating data-driven decision-making in urban renewal projects.

o Utilizing generative AI models for predictive modeling of urban development patterns, aiding in the identification of sustainable and livable urban environments.

97. Venture Capital:

o Utilizing generative AI for investment analysis and due diligence, assisting venture capital firms in identifying potential investment opportunities and assessing risks.

o Developing generative AI algorithms for startup valuation and portfolio optimization, aiding in investment decision-making and portfolio management.

98. Wage Administration:

o Applying generative AI models for wage benchmarking and analysis, assisting organizations in ensuring fair and competitive wage administration practices.

o Utilizing generative AI for automated wage structure design and optimization, aligning wages with market standards and organizational goals.

99. Warehousing:

o Utilizing generative AI for inventory optimization and demand forecasting in warehouse management, improving efficiency and minimizing stockouts.

o Applying generative AI algorithms for automated picking and routing optimization, enhancing order fulfillment and reducing operational costs.

100. Waste Management:

o Developing generative AI models for waste sorting and recycling optimization, improving waste management processes and reducing environmental impact.

o Applying generative AI for predictive analytics in waste collection scheduling and route optimization, optimizing resource allocation and operational efficiency.

101. Website Design:

o Utilizing generative AI for automated website layout and design generation, assisting businesses in creating visually appealing and user-friendly websites.

o Applying generative AI models for personalized website content recommendation and optimization, improving user engagement and conversion rates.

102. Winery Management:

o Developing generative AI models for vineyard analytics and grape quality prediction, aiding wineries in optimizing grape cultivation and harvest decisions.

o Utilizing generative AI for wine quality assessment and recommendation, assisting wineries in product development and quality control.

103. Writing:

- o Applying generative AI for automated content generation, assisting businesses in producing high-quality and engaging written content at scale.
- o Utilizing generative AI models for language generation and style adaptation, aiding writers in maintaining consistent tone and style across various writing projects.

Remember, the application of generative AI to these areas requires domain expertise in the specific consulting field and a deep understanding of AI technologies. **A consultant with knowledge in both areas** can provide valuable insights and solutions tailored to the client's needs and objectives.

Appendix 3

GEN AI Industry-Specific Example "Drill-downs" – Prompt Methodology

Example GPT-driven Drill-downs:

Initial Prompts: Strategy Consulting

- Applying generative AI for strategic decision-making, such as generating alternative scenarios and evaluating their potential outcomes.
- Utilizing generative AI models to simulate and optimize business strategies based on different variables and constraints.

1st Drill-down:

Here's more detail regarding the application of *generative AI in Strategy Consulting*:

1. Applying generative AI for strategic decision-making:

    o Generative AI can assist in strategic decision-making by generating alternative scenarios and evaluating their potential outcomes. By using generative AI models, consultants can simulate various business scenarios, considering different variables and market conditions. This allows for a comprehensive assessment of the potential risks and rewards associated with different strategic choices.

    o For example, generative AI models can generate simulations that explore the impact of market fluctuations, competitive dynamics, and customer behavior on business performance. Consultants can leverage these simulations to make informed decisions about market entry strategies, product portfolio management, resource allocation, and other strategic choices.

o   Utilizing generative AI models to simulate and optimize business strategies:

o   Generative AI models can simulate and optimize business strategies based on different variables and constraints. Consultants can utilize these models to test various strategic options and identify the most effective approach.

o   For instance, generative AI can be used to simulate pricing strategies and assess their impact on revenue and market share. Consultants can input different pricing scenarios, market demand patterns, and competitive dynamics into the generative AI models to evaluate the potential outcomes of each strategy. This allows for data-driven decision-making and optimization of pricing strategies to maximize profitability.

2.   Furthermore, generative AI models can assist in optimizing other strategic elements, such as supply chain management, distribution strategies, and marketing campaigns. By running simulations and considering different constraints and objectives, consultants can identify the most efficient and effective strategies for their clients.

In summary, generative AI can play a significant role in Strategy Consulting by providing powerful tools for strategic decision-making and optimization. By applying generative AI, consultants can generate alternative scenarios, simulate strategic choices, and evaluate their potential outcomes. This enables data-driven decision-making and helps businesses develop and optimize their strategies to achieve their goals.

2nd Drill-down:

For detailed statistics and references on the specific application of generative AI in strategy consulting, we recommend referring to research papers, industry reports, and academic journals in the field of artificial intelligence, machine learning, and management consulting. These sources often provide empirical evidence, case studies, and references to support the application of generative AI in strategic decision-making and optimization.

Some reputable sources to explore for further information on the topic include:

Academic Journals:

Harvard Business Review

Strategic Management Journal

Journal of Management Consulting

Journal of Business Strategy

Journal of Artificial Intelligence Research

Industry Reports and Publications:

McKinsey & Company: "The AI-powered organization"

Deloitte: "AI-powered strategic planning for business growth"

Gartner: "Using AI to Drive Strategic Business Planning"

These sources often provide insights, case studies, and references to support the application of generative AI in strategy consulting. Additionally, consulting firms, research institutions, and technology companies involved in AI and management consulting publish reports and articles on this topic.

When exploring these sources, be sure to look for studies or reports specific to generative AI and its application in strategy consulting. This will help you find more detailed information, statistics, and references to support your research on the subject.

Auto Sales Training Consulting Drill-down:

Here we can first provide you with general insights on the benefits of sales training based on industry observations and studies in the field of sales and training. It is important to note that the impact of sales training can vary depending on various factors such as the quality of the training program, the skills and motivation of the sales team, and the market conditions. Here are some general points highlighting the potential effects of good sales training in automobile sales:

Increased Sales Performance:

Effective sales training can enhance the skills and knowledge of salespeople, enabling them to engage customers more effectively, identify needs, and address objections. This can result in improved sales performance, including higher conversion rates, increased average deal size, and improved customer satisfaction.

Enhanced Customer Experience:

Sales training can equip salespeople with the tools and techniques to provide a better customer experience. By understanding customer needs, actively listening, and offering personalized recommendations, salespeople can build trust, establish strong relationships, and create positive experiences for potential buyers.

Improved Product Knowledge:

Sales training programs that focus on product knowledge can help salespeople understand the features, benefits, and competitive advantages of the vehicles they sell. This enables them to provide accurate and compelling information to customers, answer questions effectively, and highlight the value proposition of the dealership's offerings.

Enhanced Sales Techniques:

Sales training can introduce or reinforce effective sales techniques, such as objection handling, negotiation skills, and closing strategies. These techniques empower salespeople to navigate customer objections, address concerns, and guide customers towards making a purchase decision.

Adaptability to Changing Market Conditions:

Good sales training can help salespeople adapt to evolving market conditions, changing customer preferences, and new technologies. Training programs that incorporate industry trends, market insights, and customer behavior analysis can ensure sales teams are equipped to meet the demands of a dynamic and competitive automotive market.

Improved Team Collaboration:

Sales training programs that encourage teamwork and collaboration can foster a positive sales culture within the dealership. By promoting knowledge sharing, best practices, and a supportive sales environment, training can improve team dynamics and enhance overall sales performance.

While the specific impact of sales training on automobile sales can vary, investing in high-quality training programs and continuous development for sales teams has the potential to deliver significant benefits. It is always recommended for automotive dealerships to evaluate their specific training needs, consider industry best practices, and monitor the outcomes of their sales training initiatives to measure the effectiveness of the training efforts.

Now, here's a more specific recommendation for automobile sales training *consulting* and how a consultant could assist a dealership *by leveraging generative AI tools:*

1. Personalized Sales Training Programs:

    o   The consultant can develop personalized sales training programs using generative AI tools tailored to the specific needs of the dealership's sales team. These programs can consider factors such as individual skill levels, experience, and areas for improvement.

    o   Generative AI models can analyze the performance data of each salesperson, identify their strengths and weaknesses, and generate personalized training content accordingly. This content may include interactive modules, multimedia resources, and simulated sales scenarios.

2. Virtual Sales Simulations:

    o   The consultant can leverage generative AI tools to create virtual sales simulations that mimic real-world sales interactions. These simulations can provide a safe and controlled environment for salespeople to practice and refine their sales techniques.

    o   Generative AI models can simulate different customer personas and buying scenarios, allowing salespeople to engage in realistic sales conversations and receive instant feedback on their performance. This feedback can highlight areas for improvement and suggest effective sales strategies.

3. Customer Profiling and Targeting:

o The consultant can use generative AI tools to analyze customer data and generate detailed customer profiles. These profiles can include information such as demographics, preferences, and buying behaviors.

o Generative AI models can help identify high-potential customer segments for the dealership's vehicles. By understanding customer preferences and needs, salespeople can tailor their approach and product recommendations to enhance customer engagement and increase the likelihood of making a sale.

4. Sales Process Optimization:

o The consultant can assist the dealership in optimizing their sales process by leveraging generative AI tools. These tools can analyze historical sales data, identify bottlenecks, and suggest process improvements.

o Generative AI models can provide real-time guidance to salespeople during the sales process. This guidance can include tips, objection handling strategies, and upselling opportunities based on the customer's profile and behavior.

5. Pricing Strategy Optimization:

o The consultant can utilize generative AI tools to optimize the dealership's pricing strategy. These tools can analyze market trends, competitor pricing, and customer demand to identify the optimal pricing for different vehicle models and customer segments.

o Generative AI models can simulate pricing scenarios and evaluate their impact on sales volume and profitability. This information can help the dealership determine the most effective pricing strategies to maximize revenue and maintain a competitive edge.

6. Performance Analytics and Reporting:

o The consultant can leverage generative AI tools to analyze sales performance data and generate comprehensive reports and dashboards. These tools can track key performance indicators (KPIs), such as conversion rates, average deal size, and customer satisfaction.

o   Generative AI models can provide insights into sales team performance, highlighting top performers, areas for improvement, and training needs. This information can guide coaching efforts and enable data-driven decision-making to enhance overall sales effectiveness.

By leveraging generative AI tools, a consultant can assist a dealership with their sales training by personalizing training programs, creating virtual sales simulations, optimizing the sales process, refining pricing strategies, and providing performance analytics. These generative AI-driven solutions can help sales teams improve their skills, increase customer engagement, and drive higher sales conversions in the competitive automobile sales industry.

www.ingramcontent.com/pod-product-compliance
Lightning Source LLC
LaVergne TN
LVHW051702050326
832903LV00032B/3961